THE REFERENCE SHELF   VOLUME 45 NUMBER 5

THE AMERICAN INDIAN
A RISING ETHNIC FORCE

EDITED BY

HERBERT L. MARX, JR.

THE H. W. WILSON COMPANY
NEW YORK   1973

THE REFERENCE SHELF

The books in this series contain reprints of articles, excerpts from books, and addresses on current issues and social trends in the United States and other countries. There are six separately bound numbers in each volume, all of which are generally published in the same calendar year. One number is a collection of recent speeches; each of the others is devoted to a single subject and gives background information and discussion from various points of view, concluding with a comprehensive bibliography. Books in the series may be purchased individually or on subscription.

Copyright © 1973

By The H. W. Wilson Company

PRINTED IN THE UNITED STATES OF AMERICA

Library of Congress Cataloging in Publication Data

Marx, Herbert L   comp.
  The American Indian: a rising ethnic force.

  (The Reference shelf, v. 45, no. 5)
  Bibliography: p.
  1. Indians of North America--Addresses, essays,
lectures. 2. Indians of North America--Government
relations--1934-   --Addresses, essays, lectures.
I. Title. II. Series.
E77.2.M37   970.1   73-16444
ISBN 0-8242-0508-1

PREFACE

The story of the American Indian, until quite recently, has been a passive one. The Indian was someone to whom something was done. He was—the list is endless—defeated in battle, forced to move, relocated to a reservation, restricted in his rights, then carefully "given" rights, educated separately and certainly not equally, and even carefully set in the proper pose for a tourist's photograph.

Today there is a new, exciting, active story to tell. In sheer numbers, the American Indian population is growing at a far faster rate than the general population. That is the less significant fact. What counts is a new recognition of the Indian as a self-propelled, free-minded, creative force in American society, as never before.

Much of this is a natural development, the logical result of years of survival in the face of adversity and of cultural strength and undying faith in a way of life. What has no doubt accelerated the change in the status of the American Indian is the stage-center appearance of many other groups in American society, seeking and demanding a new status—blacks, youth, women (in a "liberated" sense), Chicanos and others. In this context, it became fashionable to refer to Indians as the "native Americans" or the "first Americans." Was not the name *Indian* after all, given to natives of this land by European explorers mistaken in their belief that this land was the East Indies? Should not *Indian* take the same place in history as the reference to black people as *Negroes*?

Yet somehow "native American" has not caught on. The "Indian" seems content to be called just that. More important, there is a surprise in store for those who would liberate or assimilate or integrate the Indian, even with the highest of motives. The surprise is that Indians—or, to avoid a stereotyping error, most Indians—want nothing of the sort. It is not strange, when one reflects on it, that they feel secure in the place and the setting which were theirs for many centuries before the white man arrived. They want to preserve their rights, they desperately seek redress for the wrongs which have been visited upon them. But beyond that? Beyond that is the stuff of which this volume is composed: The variety among tribes complicates the problems of the ongoing revolution, as does the relationship of these tribes with the Federal Government and particularly the beleaguered Bureau of Indian Affairs. Education and urbanization, furthermore, point up the dilemma of preserving Indian culture in a technological society. Indeed, the survival of the Indian way of life has a direct bearing on the future of all America. Summed up, the material presented here is a call to look at this force within our society in the terms of the 1970s—the active, not the passive, Indian.

As is stressed in this book, there are many kinds of Indian tribes, many different varieties of Indian cultures and aspirations, just as there are many different types of people and societies within, say, the continent of Europe. Generalizations about Indians, like most generalizations, must be made with care.

Yet one can be made: within every Indian culture there has been the good sense to apply a primal belief in the need to live with nature and to preserve the surroundings and resources which nurture and sustain mankind. In today's world of impending ecological crises—if not disasters—the way of the Indian is more and more frequently observed as perhaps the only possible long-range solution for man's viability on earth.

In sum, this book attempts to reflect changing attitudes—both of and toward Indians. In a world of terrorism, turmoil, mistrust, and discontent, the American Indians and their role as a rising influence on American life may be one of the most welcome sociological developments of the decade.

The editor wishes to express his appreciation to Joan Munster for her patient and efficient assistance and to the publishers and authors who have permitted the reproduction of materials in this volume.

HERBERT L. MARX, JR.

September 1973

CONTENTS

I. A BACKGROUND OF MANY HUES

EDITOR'S INTRODUCTION

Until quite recently scant attention was paid to the American Indian, except in the context of the history of the United States or as the follower of a colorful and fascinating life style. Now, however, it is newly apparent to most Americans that the Indian's role is at once a changing and yet stolidly unchanging part of the national panorama.

The description of the role of Indians in American society is increasingly being related by Indians themselves, as evidenced by two of the articles in this introductory section, as well as in many other selections throughout this volume. In addition, many non-Indian social scientists are presenting authoritative portraits of the many facets of Indian life.

In the first article in this section, Dr. Murray L. Wax, a noted sociologist, presents an overview of the diversity of the "native peoples of the Americas." The general review is continued by Franklin Dusheneaux, a congressional counsel and Cheyenne-River Sioux Indian, as he looks beyond the stereotypes of the usual impressions concerning native Americans.

Two news reviews summarize the status of Indians and their goals today. They are followed by a strong expression of opinion by Professor John Greenway, an anthropologist, who takes a position quite contrary to the current consensus about Indians. Finally, Rupert Costo, president of the American Indian Historical Society, exhorts his fellow Indian scholars to further "true Indian values" and their "deep and profound goals."

WHO IS AN INDIAN? [1]

Throughout the Americas—North, South, and Central —are millions of peoples who are referred to as Indians. In the past (and still today) most of these peoples did not refer to themselves by this word, but instead labeled themselves as members of small bands or villages of kith and kin. In like manner, the peoples who inhabited Europe during the Middle Ages would not have referred to themselves as "European" or "French" or "German," but instead would have spoken in terms of their membership in a family household and their residence in a local region. The categories of being *white* (European), or *black* (African), or *Indian* (native American) were to come about as a consequence of the exploration, trade, conquest, and settlement which brought the Europeans into intimate and prolonged contact with other peoples of the world. This expansion is typified by Christopher Columbus, and it was he, seeking a direct route to "the Indies" (i.e., Southeast Asia), who labeled the American natives as *los Indios*. The Spanish conquistadores who accepted his geographic conjectures and followed his routes also continued his nomenclature, and so the native Americans acquired their name of *Indian*.

To the social scientist, the native peoples of the Americas have appeared markedly diverse. For example, in linguistic terms, the native languages can be classed into about a dozen stocks (each as distinct from the other as the Semitic from the Indo-European), and within each stock into languages as distinct as English from Russian, so the Americas were linguistically as diverse as the Euroasian land mass. (Most of the classifications of Indians into tribes, nations, or peoples have been linguistic, e.g., Siouan, Iroquoian, Athapaskan, rather than political, e.g., the Six Nations.) Likewise, the Indians have been heterogeneous in their level of native technology and complexity of social organization, ranging

[1] From *Indian Americans: Unity and Diversity*, by Murray L. Wax, department of sociology, University of Kansas. Prentice-Hall. '71. p 3-5, 32-4. © 1971. Reprinted by permission of Prentice-Hall, Inc., Englewood Cliffs, New Jersey.

from the large and civilized societies of Central America and the Andes (Maya, Aztec, Inca) to the small and relatively primitive societies of the Paiute, Seri, or Fuegian. That the Spanish and other European invaders could perceive this diversity as a unity, and so maintain the single term *Indian* is significant of a constancy of relationship. Regardless of the heterogeneity both of the invaders from Europe and of the natives of the Americas, the pattern of their relationship was to prove so constant that it could be characterized as a confrontation of *Indian* and *white*. . . . To seek a parallel elsewhere, we can note how the slave trade transformed the Ibo, Hausa, Yoruba, and other peoples of the African west coast into simply *Negroes* (the Spanish term for *black*). . . .

There have been significant differences in the ways that whites and Indians related to each other. In some cases, the invaders sought to exterminate the natives—sometimes simply to rid the land of troublesome tenants, and sometimes for the sport of hunting a human quarry. At other times, the invaders sought to assimilate the natives by Christianizing them or forcibly detribalizing them (through religious missions, compulsory schooling in isolation from their kin, and economic sanctions). Frequently the natives were driven and corraled into regions of the country which the invaders had found unsuitable for their own settlement and exploitation. Meanwhile, there was interbreeding that was sometimes sanctioned as concubinage or even marriage. There were even handfuls of whites who settled among Indians and found the native ways so congenial that they assimilated, and hundreds of thousands of Indians have assimilated into the national society of their locality.

Given the original diversity of the natives of the Americas and the varieties of treatment to which they have been subjected, there is a problem in deciding who or what group should be categorized as *Indian*. For example, in terms of descent, there have been a number of eminent figures in US life with a significant degree of Indian blood in their veins, e.g., Will Rogers, the humorist; Jim Thorpe, the ath-

lete; Maria Tallchief, prima ballerina assoluta; and Jack
Dempsey, the prizefighter; not to mention corporation executives, political leaders, and the like. In Central and South
America, it is equally true that many prominent men have
had some or considerable Indian ancestry. Yet, in all areas
of the Americas, one basic referent of *Indian* has come to
mean the enclaves or bands who are culturally unique and
socially isolated. In Peru, Venezuela, and many other Latin
American countries, *los Indios* are the politically impotent,
economically impoverished, culturally traditional, and socially enclaved groups who do not participate in the Hispanicized life of the national society. The participants in that
society view the *Indio* as an inferior beast in contrast to the
Mestizo (who bears Indian blood in his veins but has become
Hispanicized). Even within the United States, the tendency
in many regions is to denote by *Indian* not those who are of
Indian descent yet successful by the standards of the national
society, but only those who are impoverished and ethnically
distinct. Thus, many Dakotans use *Indian* to denote Sioux
they perceive as poor and "backward," while northeastern
Oklahomans use *Indian* in the same perception of Tribal
Cherokee. This should alert us to the fact that, as a word
in ordinary language, *Indian* (or *Indio*) sometimes refers
to a distinct ethnic group but more often refers to a series
of social processes of an invidious character. . . .

The aboriginal population of the region which was to
become the USA has been estimated as low as one million
and as high as ten million persons. . . . From a biological
or genetic perspective, Indians made a significant contribu-
tion to the total gene pool of US population, since much
interbreeding occurred and many of the offspring merged
into the non-Indian population, either as whites, Negroes,
or the small groups of "almost whites" that have dotted the
southern landscape. Moreover, many of the Spanish-speaking
peoples who migrated to the United States from Mexico were
largely of Indian extraction.

If, however, we speak of Indian in the sense of socially distinct bands bearing a recognizably Indian culture, then the depopulation was catastrophic. By 1800 the native population was about 600,000, and fifty years later it was about 250,000. The causes were basically malnutrition and disease, with the former predisposing to the latter. The malnutrition was caused by the eroding of the ecological basis of Indian subsistence, while the diseases were consequent upon the white migrations, including especially smallpox and tuberculosis, but also influenza, mumps, and diphtheria. The decimation of the Plains Indian tribes is well documented. For example, a smallpox pandemic in 1837 reduced the Mandan from 1,600 to 31. In addition to starvation and disease, deliberate massacres were also a major factor. In a short span of years in California—it is believed—the miners eliminated nine tenths of the original population. . . .

Indian administration in the era after the Civil War was rife with corruption, which meant that the tribes received less than the stipulated quantities of treaty goods and little in the way of health or welfare services. The plight of these peoples could not be hidden, and in time various reform associations took up the cause of the Indians. By the turn of the century there had begun some definite improvements. Correspondingly, the population of these tribes began to rise, so that in the half-century from 1910 to 1960 it has about doubled. Deliberate slaughter and debauchery had been ended, while more adequate diet, proper sanitation, and medical care have all contributed to positive growth of population.

As always, any figures on Indian population must be viewed in the context of the definition being used. For example, figures maintained by the Bureau of Indian Affairs . . . issue out of its legal responsibilities as defined by law. While the BIA inherited a custodial and even authoritarian role in relationship to Indian peoples, the legal basis for much of its operations has been its status as trustee for reservation lands, so that the peoples it is concerned with are those who qualify as owners and heirs to this land. Heirship, in turn, is determined by Anglo-Saxon principles of descent, rather than possession of cultural traits or participation in the life of an Indian community. Thus, in the strictest sense, the BIA regards as an Indian any person who qualifies as an heir to reservation land, a qualification expressed in hereditary terms as *degree of Indian blood*. In cases where a land base does not exist—as where Congress has allotted the reservation area in severalty [in separate, independent ownership] and terminated federal responsibilities—the BIA has small basis for action or responsibility. For example, the independent Cherokee Nation in northeastern Oklahoma was dissolved by act of Congress early in this century, its lands allotted in severalty, and its rolls of membership closed. Despite the fact that traditional Cherokee communities have continued to exist, maintaining the native language for domestic and ceremonial purposes, there was in 1969 neither an official roster of their population nor even any census of their numbers.

A different sort of estimate of Indian population derives from the operations of the United States Bureau of Census, but here too there have been great variations in procedures used and much leeway allowed to the census taker. Moreover, since there have been social and political disabilities connected with being classified as an Indian, many individuals of Indian ancestry have had considerable incentive to "pass" as non-Indian. In principle, intermarriage, interbreeding, and adoption of Euroamerican traits (such as style of grooming and shearing the hair) was supposed to transform the Indian into the non-Indian, and many of those who underwent such transformations did not appear on public records as *Indian*. It is arguable that if the United States counted a person as Indian in a manner parallel to that which counts him as Negro—i.e., some minimal degree of Indian ancestry, a drop of "Indian blood"—then the "Indian population" would number into the millions. In recent years there has been a considerable swing in this direction, inasmuch as a variety of advantages—economic, political, and even social—have begun to accrue to those classified as *Indian*.

Most significantly, there has been passage of legislation and establishment of a special court of claims under which Indian tribes could sue the United States Government for such past violations of civil law as taking their land for insufficient compensation. When judgments are made for an Indian tribe as plaintiff, the proceeds are distributed on an heirship basis. While the mode of handling and distributing these awards has varied, it can happen that individuals share in them who are only marginally Indian in ancestry, and not at all so in their traits or social life. In like manner, there are some federal benefits, such as access to the Indian branch of the Public Health Service, which are available to individuals who can demonstrate that they have a quarter degree or more of Indian blood. Finally, claiming to be *Indian* now has a certain cachet in many circles, even though there are hotels, restaurants, and taverns in some Western towns which make a practice of denying service to clientele that is identifiably Indian.

THE INDIAN AS CITIZEN [2]

In the nineteenth century, the white man's image of the American Indian was either that of the noble savage or the bloodthirsty, dirty redskin. The Indian in the first image could not open his mouth without having gems of great wisdom and profound philosophy pouring out in the most poetical, oratorical style. The second Indian was not happy unless he was dripping with the blood of a white man and holding aloft a scalp of flowing blond hair. Neither of these two extreme images was accurate.

[2] From "The American Indian: Beyond the Stereotypes," by Franklin Dusheneaux, Cheyenne-River Sioux; counsel, Subcommittee on Indian Affairs, United States House of Representatives Committee on Interior and Insular Affairs. *Today's Education*. 62:22-4. My. '73. Reprinted by permission.

In the twentieth century, two different images have developed in the minds of white Americans. In one—the movie/TV image—the Indian is still pictured as the mighty warrior in majestic headdress, attacking the wagon train or making fervent love to a dusky young Indian maiden. In the other, he is the sullen, broken spirit who drinks cheap wine and lives on the handouts of a sometimes benign, sometimes malicious Federal Government. These images are also inaccurate.

While the foregoing images still flavor white America's picture of the Indian to some extent, two new images have arisen in recent years. One is that of the sophisticated, intellectual tribal leader who wears tailor-made suits and carries an attaché case. The other is that of the militant Indian; the Red Power publicity seeker, burning buildings, taking hostages, and desperately seeking identification with Crazy Horse and Sitting Bull—the Wounded Knee image of 1973. [See "Wounded Knee," in Section II, below.] While these new images have a basis in fact, neither truly represents most American Indians. . . .

Indians are citizens of the United States and of the states in which they reside. Stating this may seem unnecessary, but the contrary idea with all of its implications still lingers in many minds. Most Indians became citizens by some act of Congress, particularly a 1924 act that made citizens of all noncitizen Indians then residing within the United States.

Most Indians alive today are considered citizens by birth. Except for certain specific exceptions, they are entitled to all the privileges and subject to all the duties of citizenship.

The Indian is entitled to the same services and benefits of the Federal Government and of his state of residence as other citizens *because* of his status as a citizen. He is entitled to all the protection of the laws of the United States and of the states. He is entitled to vote in all general and local elections, to serve on juries, and to avail himself of the judiciary machinery to secure his rights and redress of grievances. He is subject to military conscription. Indeed, in the wars of this nation, the voluntary enlistment of Indians and their bravery have been outstanding.

Like other citizens, Indians are subject to all the federal, state, and local taxes—except that property held in trust for them by the United States, income derived from that property, and transactions taking place on that property are tax exempt.

Indians living in a trust relationship (i.e., owning an interest in trust property) have certain restrictions placed upon their use of that property to which other citizens are not subject. Except in tribal relations and when they are on the reservation, Indians are subject to all the criminal and civil laws of the federal, state, and local governments. . . .

A trustee relationship exists between the United States and those Indian tribes recognized by the United States. It has been likened to the relationship that exists between a guardian and ward. However, it is *not* a guardian/ward relationship, although it has elements of that relationship.

The trust relationship is firmly based on the Constitution of the United States (implemented by a series of treaties and statutes), which gives Congress the power to regulate commerce with the Indian tribes.

The trust is most evident with respect to the land tenure on the reservations and the implications of tenure. Most of the land and related resources on an Indian reservation are held in trust by the United States for the beneficial use of the Indian tribe or individual. The Indian cannot sell such land or resource without the consent of the United States, and to some extent, the United States restricts other beneficial uses, such as leasing. Imposed upon the United States is a duty to protect these resources against the improvidence of the Indian and against the encroachment or avarice of outside interests.

Prior to the advent of the non-Indian on this continent, the Indian tribes were true sovereign nations. The European colonial powers, the colonies, and the United States recognized and dealt with them as such. However, primarily because of the superior force of arms implementing the so-called manifest destiny of the United States, there began a slow but increasing erosion and limitation of tribal sovereignty. To paraphrase the Supreme Court, the United States extended its dominion over this continent by the might of the sword, and the right of conquest gives a title that the courts of the conqueror cannot deny.

Implied in the foregoing paragraph is this basic tenet of Indian law: The right of might has given the United States power to limit or abolish tribal sovereignty and self-government; but except as so expressly limited or abolished, Indian tribes retain their inherent right to tribal sovereignty and self-government. The corollary of this tenet is that those sovereign rights of self-government are not grants of rights from the United States but a retention of rights inherent in the Indian tribes.

Within the boundaries of the Indian reservations, tribal government exists today. In many respects, these governments resemble those found in the counties and municipalities of this nation. Most tribal governments have legislative, executive, and judicial machinery, many based on the Anglo-Saxon model. Members of the tribes elect representatives by secret ballot. Except as limited by the United States, Indian governments exercise criminal jurisdiction over the conduct of their members. They regulate the internal affairs of their members, and, except as limited by the United States, control the use and disposition of property within their jurisdiction.

Tribal governments have the power to impose taxes and license activity. In most respects, their powers are independent of the states and surrounding local communities and governments. Such normal governmental services as road construction and maintenance, education, welfare and social services are carried on and funded by the Federal Government simply because the tribes lack funds and resources. In short, the tribes have all the sovereignty and rights of self-government that have not been expressly limited by the United States.

GOALS OF A RESTLESS PEOPLE [3]

Reprinted from *U.S. News & World Report.*

Facts About American Indians

Number: 792,730 in 1970—and increasing at a faster rate than the US population.

Tribes: About a third are either Navajo, Cherokee, Sioux or Chippewa. The Navajo tribe, making up 13 per cent of all Indians, is the biggest.

Location: About half live in the West, a fourth in the South. Oklahoma, Arizona, California, New Mexico and North Carolina have the largest Indian populations.

Dwelling: More than half 55 per cent live in rural areas, largely on reservations. One in five lives in central cities, one in four in suburbs or smaller cities.

Income: $1,115 per person on reservations, about a third of the US average. Counting all Indians, median family income is about half the US average of $11,200, about four fifths as large as the average of Negro families.

Life expectancy: 64 years at birth, compared with 70.5 years for all Americans.

Infant mortality: About 24 per cent higher than the US average.

Unemployment: 40 per cent of all Indians on reservations above age sixteen.

Source: Census Bureau, Dept. of Interior,
Office of Management and Budget

From the brown, rolling hills of the Sioux Nation in South Dakota to the Atlantic and Pacific coasts, America's Indians are heading for a showdown with federal authority over old grievances and new hopes.

[3] From "Real Goals of the Restless Indians." *U.S. News & World Report.* 74:26-30. Ap. 2, '73.

In some places, such as Wounded Knee, South Dakota, which militants seized in . . . February [1973], Indians have resorted to violence. The conflict also is going on in courthouses, in state legislatures, and in federal offices in Washington as Indian militants fight with a vigor rarely displayed since battles with the US cavalry a century ago.

There is no organized "Indian nation" in a political sense. Differences exist between tribes as well as between the well-to-do and poor, old and young, and rural and city Indians.

Despite disagreement about how the battle should be fought, widespread support is developing for basic aims, including:

Self-determination of tribes. Indians on many reservations want the power to tax, educate and police their people, and apportion resources as they see fit. Federal and state agencies now handle many of those functions.

Fulfillment of federal obligations. Indians, for example, want to regain some lands and be compensated for other properties they say were illegally wrested from them despite treaty guarantees of permanent possession.

Assurances of equal civil rights. Indians say they often are abused by law-enforcement officers and treated unfairly by the courts.

More federal money in fields such as medicine and education. Some leaders believe it will take billions of dollars from the United States Treasury to lift Indians from poverty.

A shake-up of United States Government policies dealing with Indians. Proposals range from eliminating the Bureau of Indian Affairs—which runs many programs on most reservations—to turning that organization over to an Indian-elected directorate.

At the same time, assurances are being demanded that Indians will be allowed to pursue their own way of life, culture and religion on the reservations, instead of being forced to conform to white-dictated standards.

From the late nineteenth century until recently, most Indians seemed to accept their lot fatalistically—showing no inclination to revolt.

Today, as an aftermath to the activities of black militants and other "rights" groups that have sprung up nationwide, Indians are on the move again.

Declares a Navajo in Arizona: "We're tired of people telling us what is good for us. We don't want any handouts. We want to be self-sustaining citizens of this country, but we want to do it in our own way."

A large number of Indians—tribal leaders say a vast majority—deplore the violence that has occurred at Wounded Knee. But many nonmilitants applaud the goals of such groups as the American Indian Movement (AIM), which directed the armed seizure of the hamlet.

An old Sioux woman in South Dakota says most tribal people share a common aim: "They want to be able to say, 'I'm an Indian,' and be proud of it—and respected for it, too."

President Nixon in 1970 responded to growing pressures by proposing to give Indians a substantial degree of self-determination on the reservations. [See "The President's Recommendations," in Section III, below.] Mr. Nixon also recommended stepped-up spending in many fields of Indian activity, including health-care and economic projects. These measures were not approved by Congress. Furthermore, critics say, changes were slowed down by Administration inertia and opposition from strong land, power and mining interests in the West.

After the take-over of the Bureau of Indian Affairs Building in Washington by militants in November 1972, the Government reshuffled the top leadership in the agency and promised closer contacts between the tribes and the Administration. The militants say such measures are insufficient. . . .

About That "Trail of Broken Treaties"

In the first one hundred years of nationhood, the United States concluded 389 treaties with Indian tribes, according to US records.

Today, Indian militants are using the phrase, "The Trail of Broken Treaties," to dramatize their claim that the Government consistently has broken promises made to Indians about lands and services they were to get.

The phrase, Indian spokesmen say, actually applies to all commitments formally made by the United States to the Indian people—including laws passed by Congress and presidential orders that have replaced treaties in recent times.

Much of the Indians' bitterness, however, flows from what they regard as violations of treaties concluded between 1778 and 1871.

Historians point out that for many years treaties between the fledgling republic and powerful Indian tribes were pacts between powers of near equality.

It was just two years after the signing of the Declaration of Independence, for instance, when a treaty of peace and friendship was signed with the Delaware Nation of the Ohio Valley region. This pact's aim was to help secure the Western frontier against raids by British-paid tribesmen.

Later treaties not only designated lands to be reserved to the signatory tribes, but also promised services and amenities to reservation dwellers.

An example is the 1820 "Treaty of Friendship, Limits and Accommodation Between the United States of America and the Choctaw Nation."

In setting boundaries of lands "ceded" to Choctaws in Mississippi, the United States promised:

> For the purpose of aiding and assisting the poor Indians . . . and to enable them to do well and support their families, the Commissioners of the United States engage on behalf of said States to give to each warrior a blanket, kettle, rifle gun, bullet mold and nippers, and ammunition sufficient for hunting and defense for one year. . . .

A blacksmith shall also be settled amongst them at a point most convenient to the population and a faithful person appointed whose duty it shall be to use every reasonable exertion to collect all the wandering Indians belonging to the Choctaw Nation upon the land hereby provided for their permanent settlement.

In 1871, Congress passed a statute declaring that "no Indian nation or tribe is to be recognized as a power with whom to make a treaty."

That law did not apply to existing treaties.

Even before then, primary authority for negotiating treaties with Indians had passed from the War Department, where it had been placed in 1784, to the Office of Commissioner for Indian Affairs.

This officeholder also directed the Bureau of Indian Affairs in the Department of the Interior.

For several years after 1871, the Interior department concluded agreements with tribes, subject to Senate ratification.

The last one was made in 1888 with the Columbia and Colville tribesmen in the Pacific Northwest.

Since then, it has been the Congress and the President who have had the responsibility for making basic commitments to the Indian people and their tribes.

OUR POOREST MINORITY [4]

The Bureau of the Census [has] offered statistical evidence . . . that American Indians are the poorest minority in the country.

A bureau report showed that Indians lagged behind the rest of the nation in just about every socio-economic barometer, based on the 1970 census.

The report, composed merely of statistics, coincided with a study by the United States Commission on Civil Rights,

[4] From "Census Statistics Indicate Indians Are the Poorest Minority Group," by Paul Delaney, staff correspondent. New York *Times*. p 14. Jl. 17, '73. © 1973 by The New York Times Company. Reprinted by permission.

published in May [1973], that concluded that Indians were
worse off than any other minority. The commission's study
was of Indians in New Mexico and Arizona and attributed
the problems to the Federal Government.

[The July 16, 1973] . . . census report said that the median
income of Indian families was $5,832 in 1969, against the
national median of $9,590. Further, nearly 40 per cent of
the Indian population lived below the Federal poverty level
in 1969, against 13.7 per cent of the total population.

The $5,832 median income for Indians in 1969 was less
than the $6,191 for all minorities, including the $5,999 for
blacks.

The census report noted that in thirty metropolitan
areas with at least 2,500 Indians, median family income
ranged from as low as $3,389 in Tucson, Arizona, to more
than $10,000 in Washington, D.C., and Detroit. However,
the range was lower on reservations, from $2,500 on the
Papago Reservation in Arizona to $6,115 on the Laguna
Reservation in New Mexico. . . .

The Census Bureau report . . . indicated that the only
bright spot for Indians was in education. The report showed
that 95 per cent of Indian children from seven to thirteen
years old and more than half the Indians from three to
thirty-four were attending school in 1970, and the number
attending college doubled between 1960 and 1970.

Indians in Washington, D.C., ranked above the national
averages in both median number of school years completed,
12.6, and in the percentage of high school graduates, 66. On
the other hand, the median school years completed on the
Navajo Reservation, the largest, was 4.1, and only 17 per
cent of persons there twenty-five and over had finished high
school.

Nationally, one third of all Indians over twenty-five had
completed high school, compared with less than one fifth in
1960, and median schooling was 9.8 years, the same as for
blacks. The national median was 12.1 years, and 52.3 per
cent of the total population had finished high school. . . .

The census survey showed further that 55 per cent of the Indians over sixteen years old worked in urban areas, with 70 per cent of the males employed in four broad categories—craftsmen and foremen, operatives, laborers and service workers. Only 9 per cent of Indians worked in technical and professional jobs.

A CONTRARY VIEW [5]

The lay reader should have a hardcore course in what the real Indian was like before exposing his raw conscience to . . . [recent books on American Indians]. He should know that the real Indian was ferocious, cruel, aggressive, stoic, violent, ultra-masculine, treacherous and warlike, though these are anemic adjectives to describe the extent of his Dionysiac extremism. As for our treatment of the Indians, never in the entire history of the inevitable displacement of hunting tribes by advanced agriculturists in the 39,000 generations of mankind has a native people been treated with more consideration, decency and kindness. The Mongoloids in displacing the first comers of Asia, the Negroes in displacing the aborigines in Africa, and every other group following the biological law of the Competitive Exclusion Principle thought like the Polynesian chief who once observed to a white officer: "I don't understand you English. You come here and take our land and then you spend the rest of your lives trying to make up for it. When my people came to these islands, we just killed the inhabitants and that was the end of it." It could be argued that the only real injury the white man ever did the Indian was to take his fighting away from him. Indians did not fight to defend their land, their people or their honor, as these writers apparently believe; like the Irish, they fought for the fighting. Without war and raiding and scalping and rape and pillage and slave-taking, the Indian was as aimless as a chiropractor without

[5] From "Will the Indians Get Whitey?" by John Greenway, professor of anthropology, University of Colorado. *National Review*. 21:223-8+. Mr. 11, '69. Reprinted by permission.

a spine. There was nothing left in life for him but idleness, petty mischief and booze.

Some two million people who have read Ruth Benedict's classic of just-so anthropology, *Patterns of Culture,* suppose that there were Apollonians on this earth, and that they were the Pueblo Indians. The only flaw in the Pueblos' angelic character was their effeminate peacefulness, Dr. Benedict suggested. But she did not say that the Pueblos killed the first Spaniard to visit them (ironically, the first "white" man killed by the Pueblos was a Negro), that they killed and scalped missionaries, and that they conducted the most successful of all violent Indian rebellions against the whites. . . .

As civilization displaces savagery, raiding becomes litigation. The year of 1946 will be remembered not only as the year ballpoint pens sold for $15.98, but as the year the United States was given back to the Indians. It was then that the Indian Claims Commission was quietly established by Congress as a device to simplify suits against the Government for compensation for land usurpation. In fact liability was admitted, with the only issue to be determined in most cases being which Indians should get the money. Five years were allowed for the filing of claims, and by the 1951 deadline, 852 claims were entered for 70 per cent of the United States.

This is not to say that the American conscience did not awaken until 1946. Indians have been suing the whites for more than a century and swindling them for much longer than that. The first real estate fraud on the American continent was that famous purchase of Manhattan by Peter Minuit—but the tale has been twisted over the years. It was the Dutch who were swindled; the Scaticook Indians were the occupying owners, but the deal was pulled by a mob of Canarsie Indians who were visiting Manhattan for the day. The Scaticooks, by the way, have their claim in for the island, and they are not about to take any junk jewelry for it this time.

Jefferson paid Napoleon $15 million for the Louisiana Territory in another well-publicized bargain—a sum that did not include a further $300 million under the blanket to the Indians. Some Indians were paid as many as six times for the same land, each time returning to complain that the white man was an Indian giver....

These claims do not include all the money going free from the taxpayer to the Indian. On the 397 federal reservations (eleven of which are over a million acres) no taxes are paid on either the land or its usufruct [right to use of property]—and the usufruct ran to $70 million in 1965 for rental to whites alone, not counting the uncountable hundreds of millions for primary use. And then there are the continuing service subsidies from the Bureau of Indian Affairs....

Even the Office of Economic Opportunity is shotgunning poverty funds into the Indians; in just one caper the OEO spent $208,741 to show the Zuñi how they could mass-produce their handcrafted jewelry for a guaranteed annual income of $150,000—unaware that the Zuñi already market more than $2 million worth of jewelry every year in New Mexico alone. The idea is known as "the Zany Zuñi Plan."

The Zuñi are nearly unique in that they work. Most reservation-bound Indians agree with what Chief Moses once said: "We do not want to work and don't know how. Indians are too old to learn that when five years old." The Utes are mentioned from time to time . . . as successful agriculturists, but what farming is done on the Ute reservation is done by hired white labor....

A random deskload of books all arguing the profundity of American guilt in our injustice to the Indians, and a class of students confusing American immolation with Nazi atrocities suggests a situation worth observing for the sheer insanity of it. How far can it all go? Will the 22 million Negroes in the United States sue the Government for all that free labor before 1865? Will the descendants of Adam enter a claim against the United States (God being safely dead) for their ancestor's unjust expulsion from the Garden? Will

Sioux citizen William Hawk succeed in his incredible compensation claim against the Government for wounding his
uncle, Gall, the Hunkpapa chief, when Gall led his warriors
against Custer at Little Big Horn? Will the Americans ever
find out where to go to surrender for the crime of being
Americans? Not even the Indians are safe from the implicit
absurdities of the claims game. . . . [In 1968] a suit was filed
in federal court in Denver, Colorado, against the United
States and its derivative usurpers, *including* the Indians, by
twenty-eight descendants of early Mexican grant holders.
This deprived minority claims all of California, Utah, Ore-
gon, Louisiana, Missouri, Arkansas, Iowa, North and South
Dakota, Nebraska, and Oklahoma, and parts of Kansas,
Colorado, Wyoming, Montana, Minnesota, New Mexico,
Florida, Texas, Arizona, Georgia, North and South Carolina,
Maryland, Virginia, Washington, and Idaho. Their lawyer,
a former United States Attorney for Colorado, is no ordinary
nut. A practical and reasonable man, he has indicated a
willingness to settle with the United States, the Indians and
the Civil Rights Commission for one trillion dollars. [For
another point of view, see "BIA— Friend or Foe," by Paul R.
Wieck, in Section III below.—Ed.]

MOMENT OF TRUTH [6]

This is a moment of truth for the American Indian—a
moment when we stand on the threshold of great change.
We have it in our power now to overcome the disasters of
centuries, and to perform a miracle of change in favor of a
better life for our people.

Our history in this land has a force of thousands of years'
duration, and cannot be overlooked. Our profound concern
for this land and for our people has a force so ancient and

[6] From "Moment of Truth for the American Indian," by Rupert Costo,
Cahuilla; president, American Indian Historical Society. In *Indian Voices: The
First Convocation of American Indian Scholars*. Indian Historian Press, Inc.
1451 Masonic Av. San Francisco, Calif. 94117. '70. p 3-8. Reprinted by
permission of The Indian Historian Press, American Indian Educational Publishers. Copyright 1970.

all-absorbing that it cannot be ignored. Yet we are indeed ignored and we are overlooked, in all the practical elements of life as it affects our people. Somehow, despite the many promises, and despite the many evidences of concern, the Native American lives in poverty, receives a complete and fruitful education only by the exercise of the greatest personal sacrifices, and dies in squalor....

The problems that disturb us—the issues that we need to talk about openly—the *facts of life* that beg for a meeting of our minds, these are the things we must deal with in our tribal meetings, and in our organizations, if we are to achieve our goals. We need to ask questions of ourselves, and of one another. We need to explore areas of concern, and come to mutual and unified decisions. It is not true that Indians cannot unite. We have united for years in our immense effort for sheer survival. In matters of practical need, it is enough if we can unite on a point no larger than the head of a pin, in order to make gains. In matters of the larger concern, it becomes a matter of exploration of thought and ideology, of ideas . . . and the use of creative intelligence. Let us ask ourselves some of these questions . . . questions of profound concern for ourselves as a people.

Is there, truly and honestly, anything left of our Indian cultures, traditions, and lifeways? I know there is, and you know it too. Therefore, let us pinpoint these areas of remaining Indian heritage, preserve the remaining cultures, traditions, philosophy, and the languages of our people. Indeed we have a duty to our historical heritage....

There is a tendency to vulgarize our cultures and history, even among our own people. For example, there is a class being conducted in Native History, at California State College at Hayward, in which the white students are given "cute" Indian names, are assigned to imaginary and "cute" Indian tribes, and who then conduct themselves as though they are "real Indians." This is a class taught by an *Indian*. We all know about some of the things that are taught by white teachers, degrading to our people. But when an Indian pursues this type of vulgarization, then we must stop and view the whole situation, and we must begin to teach the true history of our people, teach it with respect and scholarly interpretation both to our own people, and to the American public at large. Among us, we have been remiss with respect to our children. We should have had, long ago, practical schools for our children, to keep the languages alive, to keep the beauty of our heritage alive. It is not too late to do this even now.

Another question: Shall we allow tribal society and leadership, tribal autonomy and rights, to be wiped out? Or, shall we fight to preserve our ancient sovereign rights. The present situation, I grant you, is bad, and the present leadership in many tribes has been criticized, especially by our young people. Is it not time to make a stand, and change this situation, to change this leadership if change is needed?

If we do not improve our tribal leadership, by action of the people themselves, we are faced with total destruction of Indian life and cultures. What is left of Indian culture, when the tribal entity is gone? I ask this question of our young people who are so active on the urban front, who find it impossible to act on the tribal front, and who have forsaken their own Indian people in favor of a struggle with windmills and shadows. For, if tribal life disappears, so too does the Indian as an Indian. This is our political entity. This is what remains of our social structure and lifeways. And this is where it is *at*. In my opinion, tribal society has been deformed and degraded by the Bureau of Indian Affairs. I think this should be changed, and I think it can be changed—but only with the greatest courage and single-mindedness, and only by our young people.

Let me pose another question. . . . Shall we continue to allow our scholars, artists, and leaders to be overlooked and overshadowed, and even completely ignored by educational institutions, cultural programs, and institutional projects? Is it not time that we refuse to allow ourselves to be ex-

ploited for the sake of the self-interest of an ambitious intellectual, an ambitious city or state, or a Chamber of Commerce seeking to develop tourist attractions?

I say that we must insist, that wherever Indian programs
are considered, Indian scholars and tribal people shall be
dealt with, and shall constitute the leadership of such programs. We are continually confronted with ready-made programs that are carbon copies of programs for blacks, Chicanos
and other ethnic groups. These programs have no relationship to our history and culture, nor to our situation today,
and they are absolutely worthless, either for teaching about
Indians, or for teaching Indians themselves. . . .

The Native American population is small, compared to
that of the whole country. It would appear that efforts should
be combined, expended wisely and with the greatest promise
of effectiveness. I know there are some who have become
stupefied with the public interest, the publicity, the head-
lines. By itself, it will not solve anything. Together with a
sound program of change, it will help enormously.

Where shall we look for help, to cause a miracle of change
to happen? Certainly not from the Federal Government.
Neither the Eisenhower, the Johnson, nor to date the Nixon
Administration has developed a single effective and successful program leading to the practical improvement of our
condition. We ourselves will have to take positive and effective action to make this change possible.

In this great effort, those who are scholars, those who are
students, and those of us who are tribal activists, must unite
all our energies and talents, so that the people may once
again be the leading force in our lives and in our destiny.

Today's society is being torn apart by internal struggle.
There is destruction ahead. Already there are forces in motion, questioning the whole fabric of American society, questioning the form of government here in this country, strug-
gling and fighting—but truly they don't know for *what*, and
often they don't even know *why*. This land is rotting to

death. It is corrupt in so many ways and in so many places that water pollution is secondary to spiritual pollution.

Poverty is rampant in this nation, and the Indian is suffering most from this disease. I don't see any way to help, other than by our own people helping one another. We have to be aware of the current tumult in this land. *Every value* is being questioned, and many are already discarded like a dirty rag. The government that exists in peace today, may be confronted with questions of mere survival tomorrow. The society that has been happy with its porcelain bathtubs, its television sets, automobiles, and all the supposed comforts of life, is no longer happy to own an automobile and a television set, while also *being owned* by a finance company. In the intellectual world, the same turmoil is taking place, and perhaps even more. Because all the beliefs of western civilization are now being challenged. The honors that men receive with such gladness today, may well be the shame of tomorrow.

I think that the true Indian values, however, persist. And I am proud to know this, and to know that *my* people still hold to their spiritual life and their love of their land. I believe in their deep and profound goals. I believe that *we Indians* have more to offer this world than any other section of society.

II. "RED POWER": THE AMERICAN INDIAN REVOLUTION

EDITOR'S INTRODUCTION

"Black Power," "Power to the People," "Women's Lib," "Generation Gap": These and other current slogans reflect the growing strength and unity—real or imagined—of special groups within our society. It is inevitable, therefore, to hear the rising expression of Indian expectations dubbed as "Red Power." But, as the articles in this section indicate, "Red Power" may be a most inappropriate battle cry to describe today's American Indian "revolution." Activism, yes—just as other groups have become more active in contrast to an historical passivity. But what do *the* Indians—or more accurately *certain* Indians—want to change? Answers to that question form the substance of this section.

The section begins with two articles which examine the overall "Red Power" concept: the first by Alvin M. Josephy, Jr., one of the most respected observers of Indian affairs; the second by Beatrice Medicine, a Standing Rock Sioux. This is followed by three articles on Wounded Knee—the two-and-a-half-month "incident" which captured the nation's attention in early 1973. Was Wounded Knee a genuine action-by-violence uprising, a highly successful publicity stunt, an isolated occurrence, or a bit of all three? The *Wall Street Journal,* the New York *Times,* and a first-hand Indian observer express their views.

The final selection is a review of a special aspect of today's Indian "uprising"—the use of Indian image and culture as a symbol. The events described at Dartmouth College are but one example of the new light being shed on white society's heretofore casual judgment of the "red man."

THE NEW INDIAN PATRIOTS [1]

In 1964 some patronizing whites, wealthy do-gooders of
the kind that had long been satisfying their own frustrations
and problems by asserting possessory rights over American
Indians—"protecting" them against other whites, solving
their problems for them, and in their arrogance treating the
Indians as children who could have no idea what was best
for them in this best of all possible worlds—got the shock
of their lives.

As they had done many times before, they took a group
of Indians to New York to meet the press and other makers
of public opinion in the eastern fountainhead of American
communications so that the Indians could tell them, once
again, of the problems on the reservations. This time a bolt
of lightning struck.

The Indians were young, college-educated, articulate—
and fed up. They represented a new organization of their
own, the National Indian Youth Council, and they had a lot
to say. To the consternation of their patrons, and to the de-
light of the open-mouthed and unbelieving press, they attacked the do-gooders and told them to get off the Indians'
backs; they ridiculed their own elders, the "Uncle Tomahawks" among the tribal leaders, who for decades had sold
out the Indians by letting the do-gooders decide what was
best for their people; and they demanded Red Power—power
of the Indian people over all their own affairs.

Those young Indians, those who came to New York and
those whom they represented (and their names are already
a part of history: Clyde Warrior, a Ponca; Melvin Thom, a
Nevada Paiute; Herbert Blatchford, a Navajo; Bruce Wilkie,
a Makah from Washington state; and others) started something. They had cast off dependence on their conquerors
and oppressors; they had looked inward at the values and

[1] From *Red Power: The American Indians' Fight for Freedom*, by Alvin
M. Josephy, Jr., senior editor, American Heritage Publishing Company; author
of many books on Indian history. American Heritage. '71. p 13-15, 17-19.
Reprinted by permission.

strengths of their own peoples; and they had sounded a call for all Indians to use those strengths to establish lives for themselves on their own terms.

The slogan "Red Power" was articulated at first partly with tongue in cheek. Borrowed from "Black Power," with which black militants were already moving both blacks and whites to face each other in idea-shattering confrontations, it had an initial shock value on just the persons whom it should have shocked. The patronizers were angered by the ingratitude of their "wards" (never ones to feel particularly friendly to blacks, the do-gooders revealed their racism with such reactions as "the Indians are behaving just like the blacks"). The oppressed and desperate Indians on the reservations and the lonely and anxious ones in the cities and at white men's educational institutions sat up, took notice, and began to put pressure on the "Uncle Tomahawks" who had abdicated their responsibilities and loyalties to their peoples. And the rest of the population, with pleasure or fear—depending on their attitudes about the rights of minorities—cheered the Indians' new fighting spirit or fulminated against "Red Muslims" who were urging a race war against the whites. It took no time at all for the humor to drop away and for the coiners of the slogan, and of its equivalent, "Indian Power," to see that they had given voice to a new, and totally serious, idea and force.

Red Power, as it has been taken up in the intervening years by Indians throughout the United States (as well as in Canada), today reflects a determined and patriotic Indian fight for freedom—freedom from injustice and bondage, freedom from patronization and oppression, freedom from what the white man cannot and will not solve.

The background of this American Indian revolution—for it must be viewed as such—has been stated many times, but it is the setting for the struggle, and it should be reiterated here.

For almost five hundred years Indians have been fighting defensively for their right to exist—for their freedom, their

lands, their means of livelihood, their organizations and societies, their beliefs, their ways of life, their personal security,
their very lives. Those who still remain after so many generations of physical and cultural genocide continue to be
oppressed by shattering problems, most of them created by
the intruder, conqueror, and dispossessor—the white man. . . .

It is still widely held by the unknowing that so long as
Indians insist on being Indians and maintaining their reservations as the basis of their life, just so long will they sit in
poverty and indolence and starve. But the ranks of the more
knowledgeable among non-Indians are growing. Attracted
first to the struggle of the blacks, Americans have become
seriously attentive to the status and needs of all minorities
within the nation. The resulting new interest in Indians has
created a climate for an increase in realistic understanding
of what the Indians have been saying.

It must also be understood that the Indians themselves
have helped in creating this new climate. Increasing numbers of Indians are learning how to communicate with non-
Indians so that the latter will listen and understand. Indian
organizations are becoming stronger and more practiced in
their use of the non-Indians' communications media, and
together with the individual tribes and their leaders, and
with Indian scholars and intellectuals, they are riding the
winds of change that are abroad in today's world, demanding
and receiving the attention of the non-Indians.

In the new climate the strongest and loudest Indian
voices are those that speak selflessly and patriotically of Red
—or Indian—Power. Their numbers are swelling, particularly among the younger Indians. In substance their message
is no different from what it has been for decades, but it is
more challenging and insistent. It demands, rather than
pleads for, self-determination: the right of Indians to decide
programs and policies for themselves, to manage their own
affairs, to govern themselves, and to control their land and
its resources. It insists on the inviolability of their land and

on the strict observance and protection of obligations and rights guaranteed the Indians by treaties with the Federal Government.

There is nothing startling about any of this. For generations—until historic new federal attitudes emerged in 1970 [see "The President's Recommendations," in Section III, below]—the Indians were governed, like colonial subjects, by the Bureau of Indian Affairs of the Department of the Interior. An untrusting, sometimes corrupt, and often incompetent white man's bureaucracy, accountable in practice to Congress and the Bureau of the Budget rather than to the Indians, it exercised autocratic veto powers over all aspects of Indian life that were important to the Indians and perpetuated and spread abroad the myth that Indians were not intelligent or competent enough to manage their own affairs.

To the Bureau, as to the patronizing do-gooders, Red Power advocacy was an unsettling force. It asserted angrily that Indian peoples were, and always had been, intelligent, competent humans. Their history before the coming of the whites demonstrated that they managed their own affairs as well as, if not better than, white men were now managing the affairs of the modern, non-Indian world. Indian societies, it stated, were usually just right for the conditions and environments of the individual peoples, who protected the environment and lived in harmony with nature and the cosmos. There was no reason to believe that the Indians on their own could not once again create—better and faster than any white man could make for them— societies that harmonized with the environments in which they existed, the resources they possessed, and the limitations of the surrounding white societies. If there was a successful future that could be envisioned for Indian peoples who achieved the right of self-determination, it was of tribal groups on their own federally protected lands, which were made economically viable by Indian-determined programs. The programs—assisted, where requested, by the expertise of technicians and specialists and by adequate funding and credit—would be organized and managed by the Indians, just as non-Indians ran their own townships, counties, or other community units. The tribal lands, in this view, would be administered by and for Indians, with Indians controlling their own local governments, courts, funds, schools, and other public institutions.

Beginning in the late 1960s, the Federal Government began evidencing awareness of the Indians' growing pressure for the right of self-determination, and in 1970 President Nixon, acknowledging that the Indians should have that right, called on Congress to join him in bringing about its realization. At the same time, the Bureau of Indian Affairs, putting more Indians into top, policy-making positions, initiated long-needed structural and philosophical changes designed to make itself more responsive to the needs of the Indian people and give the tribes full opportunities to control their own affairs.

Much still remained to be done, however, in the way of implementing the new intentions, and by the end of 1970 the Indians' fight for freedom had already entered a new and more militant phase. Where Red Power advocacy had previously taken the form of demands, petitions, meetings, and with a few exceptions, demonstrations that were peaceful, a growing desperation and sense that official ears were closed and minds locked induced small but increasingly numerous groups of Indians in all parts of the country to take action on their own behalf. Alcatraz [former federal prison in San Francisco Bay] had been occupied late in 1969 as a symbol of the Indians' new determination to go on the offensive for their rights. Other organized confrontations, some successful and some not, occurred in rapid succession in New York, Michigan, South Dakota, California, Washington state, Wisconsin, Colorado, Massachusetts, and elsewhere. Although the motives differed (some were to retake land that the Indians had never ceded, some were to oust white interlopers on Indian lands, and some were to defend treaty rights), all the actions reflected a growing awareness among Indians that Red Power could be more than a slogan.

THE MANY ASPECTS OF RED POWER [2]

The first public exposure to the term *Red Power* occurred on the February 5, 1967, report of the Frank McGee Television newscast. This news item indicated that a coterie of American Indians advocated "Red Power" and were spearheading a *movement* toward independence. This appearance was an outgrowth of the National Congress of American Indians' meeting in Denver. The then Executive Director of this national Indian organization apparently sanctioned the use of "Red Power" in these terms: "to run the reservations"; "to participate in American life on our terms"; "to withdraw from everything if the tribes so wished"; and claimed that "treaties give rights." He demonstrated the use of slogans—as "We shall overcome" and "Custer died for your sins." Most importantly, it seems that this media presentation coalesced Indian sentiment to include these wants—"self-government," "not asking the bureaucrats," and "wanting larger revolving loan funds." In short, the dominant theme centered upon self-determination by native enclaves. . . .

In general, Native Americans see their position as unique. The idea of power, or of a force transcending tribal aggregates and essentially controlling the destiny of Indians, obviously had great appeal to Indians. As this new social revolution appealed to the youth of all segments of the dominant society, so, too, its appeal was great for younger Native Americans. It thus served as a rallying cry for hitherto fractionated and isolated younger Indians. As a corollary, more Indian youth were attending institutions of higher learning. More personnel was available for involvement. Many of the younger people reflected the bumper-sticker stance—"It's In to Be Indian." Quite possibly, if the new, exciting "hippie" generation was so enthralled with Native Americans as to

[2] From "Red Power, Real or Potential," by Beatrice Medicine, Standing Rock Sioux, assistant professor of anthropology, San Francisco State College. In *Indian Voices: The First Convocation of American Indian Scholars.* Indian Historian Press, Inc. 1451 Masonic Av. San Francisco, Calif. 94117. '70. p 299-307. Reprinted by permission of The Indian Historian Press, American Indian Educational Publishers. Copyright 1970.

emulate them with beaded head bands, moccasins, and an interest in peyote, what, then, was wrong with being an Indian?

Whatever the speculation about the appeal of "Red Power," its implications centered in the connotations of its dynamic and manipulative qualities. The potential of control seemed powerful, indeed. However, its positive aspects have never been universal in the Indian world. Many Indian people consider it a misnomer; some consider it as action: picketing; destroying property; capturing islands. Some consider it stupid. The more common appellation of "Red" in the sense of *Communist* is a factor also considered by more conservative Indians. No matter what dimension provides the view, "Red Power" is a term of great emotional effect, and this is especially so among the youth of many isolated reservations. . . .

"Red Power" as a diffuse concept has been seen and utilized differentially by each Indian-interest group. The *modus operandi* has been revamped to fit the immediate needs of the group. Early, the overt play of power began with strikes, fish-ins, which displayed a youthful intertribal character.

One avowedly militant group has followed the "black" pattern, with picketing, with signs, disrupting meetings, and using revolutionary rhetoric complete with four-letter words. Some students of this description have not made the transition from confrontation politics to the exacting studies, which possibly are a better step to effective power.

Another group has organized to pressure the urban community, but has been aware of the community and its imagery of Indians. It appears to be aware also of particular and peculiar Native American "habits." Essentially this awareness has been accomplished by circumventing police arrests, by patrolling urban streets for inebriated "brothers" and "sisters." Apparently, it has also ventured into homes to insure that Native Americans hit the time-clock train and get to work on time. One loosely organized group recruited Indians for the "March on Poverty" in Washington. All these groups present an intertribal group and they tend to be from all ages. The actualization of "Red Power" strikingly has caused splintering within some organizations. One youth group has devised an alternate to an either/or accommodation plan to an adjustment. It does dichotomize into reservation or assimilation polarities, which is usually the case.

This group suggests awareness of tradition and pride in Indianness as a third alternative. Additionally, the group is involved in direct social action on reservations. A further offshoot of this group is also enmeshed in reservation affairs and in "changing the community." Other splinter groups of youth have attacked the ceremonials, or the status quo, white-sponsored celebrations exploiting Indians. . . .

It is also extremely difficult to obtain data about how power is diffused, utilized and channeled in these groupings. It can be postulated that all the aforementioned devices are utilized to change "The Establishment," and effectuate decision making on the part of the Native Americans, and to display a measure of control over our destinies. Recently, the reclaiming of nonutilized federal lands is the operational framework of militancy and radicalism, or to quote an elder of mixed tribal-hyphenated background, who is at one of these places, she says, "We want to be where the action is at." Insufficient planning and extreme struggles for power and control have seriously hampered events in this area. Still the reclamation project goes on. Thus far, all projections of power have been fragmented, and organizationally and egotistically controlled.

In some instances tribal chauvinism and "provincialism" has seeped much power from actions, which have captured the public imagination and, seemingly, at the outset, cemented tribal differences.

At present the cry for Indian unity as a prelude to power seems somewhat farfetched. Self-interest of tribal groupings have provided a stultifying effect. Insufficiently utilized, it seems, is power in the political realm. Involvement by Indians in this area is not as great as it could be. This arena presents great potential. Political savvy could procure Indian participation in local, state and national affairs. Power deriving from a legal stance, clearly articulated and understood by all Indians, presents the greatest and more realistic play for power in the dominant society.

The most critical and crucial component for Indian power might be termed, for lack of a better phrase, "intellectual" power. This does not necessarily equate intellectualism with academia and/or an advanced degree. We have only to look into the diverse tribal histories of our people to point out instances of wisdom and astuteness.

This portion of power would stem from wisdom and an awareness of the structure of power in the dominant society. Additionally, constant analysis, discussions, and weighing of the many fluctuating issues in the Indian world would seem essential. Hopefully, this level of power would not be built upon personalities, but upon resilience and the ability to retreat and turn certain issues over to others more capable of handling these issues.

In the days of treaty-making the creation of chiefs was standard practice. Contemporarily, this is seen in the "House" or "Task Force Indian," who appears on countless conference agenda and government committees.

None of the previous dichotomies of "Red Power" (physical, mental, spiritual, intellectual), is mutually exclusive. However, it might appear that marching and mouthing militancy has not yielded great gains for the Native Americans. Indeed, the demand-and-reparations route might become obsolete for the Native Americans, as it seems to be doing for other minorities. Parenthetically, a complete understanding of treaties relevant to one's own tribe would provide a sounder footing for negotiations and Native decision-making and control. Underlying all of this, however, is a renewed pride of cultural heritage displayed by the contemporary Indian. A preoccupation with "identity quests" for tribal affiliation and feeling is paramount. This revitalization movement is seen in focused interest in "traditionality." Native dancing, music, art and costuming are as much a part of the reservation "pow-wow" circuit as the urban Indian "pow-wows." Subtly, but with certainty, a recharged interest in Native belief systems is evident and has great potential for fulfilling spiritual needs. . . .

Spiritual power, which might impart wisdom, compassion, understanding and concerned involvement for all Indians might also serve to circumvent tribalism of the extreme vindictive sort, which is very damaging for Indians who are concerned and working for all tribes. The common plight of the Indian entrenched in poverty and despair might also foster commitment for the physical, mental and spiritual well-being of all of us. Common bonds of "Nativeness" and "Indianness" and a touch of tolerance may eventually cause us to rise above injurious punitiveness on all levels. . . .

Potential of power to Native Americans rests upon positive self-image and a strong identity and sense of worth. Subsuming this are long entrenched tribal heritages which have withstood the ravages of war, segregation, and deliberately planned destruction of indigenous cultural systems. We may not "overcome" but we confidently and with dignity shall find our destined place in the power structure of the dominant society.

WOUNDED KNEE—I [3]

On a scrap of yellow paper pasted to a door in this town's trading post is the slogan of the "uprising" at Wounded Knee: "It is better to die on your feet than to live on your knees."

For some people, that slogan sums up the stubborn tenacity with which a band of Indians have held this hamlet since February 27 [1973]. For others, the slogan, posted where

[3] From "At Wounded Knee, Is It War or PR?" by Greg Conderacci, staff correspondent, Detroit bureau. *Wall Street Journal.* p 26. Mr. 20, '73. Reprinted with permission of *The Wall Street Journal.* © 1973 Dow Jones & Company, Inc. All Rights Reserved.

the visiting press will be able to see it, epitomizes the slick
public relations job the leaders of the militant American
Indian Movement (AIM) have done since they engineered
the takeover.

It's one of the many ironies of Wounded Knee that both
impressions are probably right. That a band of Indians
should take Wounded Knee is itself an irony—an intentional
one. Wounded Knee is the Indians' My Lai [the scene of a
massacre in Vietnam—Ed.] Almost eighty-three years ago,
more than 125 Indian men, women and children were
slaughtered here by federal troops.

The tiny town is sacred land to the Sioux and a US National Historical site. It recently received nationwide publicity in Dee Brown's best-selling book, *Bury My Heart at
Wounded Knee.* (Which takes its title from the final stanza
of Stephen Vincent Benét's poem, "American Names." "You
may bury my body in Sussex grass,/You may bury my tongue
at Champmédy./I shall not be there. I shall rise and pass./
Bury my heart at Wounded Knee.")

Clearly, for Indians, the irony lends itself to press conferences. Envision a group of Indians surrounded by armed
federals much like the Sioux of almost a century ago. The
AIM leadership did. They figured that such a scene would
capture the imagination of the American press, the American
people and even the world.

They were right. AIM succeeded in putting Wounded
Knee on the front pages of newspapers across the world and
so overcame a key problem—lack of publicity. Throughout
their history, many Indians have felt largely ignored, which
they see as a primary reason for their present plight. Since
its founding in 1968, AIM has shared that obscurity. AIM's
. . . occupation [in 1972] of the Bureau of Indian Affairs in
Washington, D.C., got the organization some visibility. But
most of its previous demonstrations, including a sit-in on
Mount Rushmore near here, have gone largely unnoticed.

That's somewhat surprising, since the AIM leaders are
master public relations men. Interviews with them are easy

to get, in contrast with the aloof federal police officials. AIM leaders are expert at rattling off catchy phrases like "If the Federal Government once again turns a deaf ear and closes its eyes to the Indian, the Indian Wars will start all over again. There will be death. I don't consider that a threat, that's reality." To aid in notetaking, Russell Means (the AIM leader who said that) will speak slowly enough for an interviewer to get every word. . . .

Tribal Disagreements

Mr. Means says he hopes the Wounded Knee takeover publicity will have a "nationalizing effect" on the Indians, convincing them they are all brothers. That isn't easy. Indians are victims of not only the white man's racism, but also of their own. Both the Indians and Bureau of Indian Affairs personnel agree there are hard feelings among Indians. Full-blooded Indians and those of mixed blood often don't get along, even within tribes. And Indians of one tribe often are at odds with Indians of other tribes. It's regarded as a positive sign by some that other Indians from outside the reservation have expressed support for one side or the other at Wounded Knee.

Another goal of the AIM leadership is to foster a badly-needed sense of pride among Indians. "We laid down our weapons at [the first] Wounded Knee," says Dennis Banks, another AIM leader. "Those weapons weren't just bows and guns, but also a sense of pride. Some of us are such sellouts that we look forward to working for the Bureau of Indian Affairs."

Even though they're not among the specific demands at Wounded Knee, AIM wants certain concessions from the Government. For one, it wants restitution for the loss of some of the vast tracts of land originally allotted . . . [the Indians] by the famous treaty of 1868. The lands include the scenic and mineral-rich Black Hills. (Other Indians have been fighting for restitution in the courts.) To achieve those goals, someone has to bargain with the Government on behalf of the Indians.

AIM would like to be that bargaining agent. That's why it occupied the Bureau of Indian Affairs in Washington. The occupation didn't yield much fruit. Mr. Means says that is because the Indians left too soon. Beyond that, the BIA building isn't a very romantic place for a takeover.

Wounded Knee, because of its history, is.

Confrontation

The occupation of Wounded Knee in the midst of the vast Pine Ridge Indian Reservation also assured that the Federal Government, which has jurisdiction over reservations, would be brought into the fray; thus, there would be a confrontation. Indeed, some observers think the Government played into the hands of the militant Indian group by responding to the challenge with blockades and other actions. (Government officials say they moved in to protect the other Sioux on the reservation.) In addition, the selection of a reservation for the conflict gave AIM, whose leadership is largely made up of Indians from outside the reservation, an opportunity to gain political power there.

Most AIM leadership are urban Indians from tribes other than the Sioux. They have attracted prominent leaders from other movements including black militant Dick Gregory. Some AIM leaders have been convicted of crimes ranging from criminal damage to property to robbery.

In order to gain the support of the Oglala Sioux on the reservation, AIM set out to exploit some dissatisfaction with the tribal president, Dick Wilson. Some Indians openly admit to fearing the alleged strong-arm tactics of the tough tribal president. AIM tried to depose the brush-cut, heavy-set Mr. Wilson, who wields considerable power on the reservation.

But the conservative Mr. Wilson, a plumber by trade, is not an easy man to move. He has already withstood chal-

lenges to his leadership, including an AIM-backed impeachment attempt. . . . And the Oglala Tribal Council, which he
heads, has voiced its overwhelming opposition to AIM a
number of times. AIM charges he is corrupt, a charge he de-
nies. If he is corrupt, he wouldn't be the first or only tribal
president to be so. But he is the top Indian on the reservation where Wounded Knee is located and so when AIM took
the tiny town, AIM demanded he be removed.

Mr. Wilson says the "crisis" at Wounded Knee is "in-
stigated by a small group of chronic complainers . . . and
certainly is causing annoyance, disgust and concern among
the overwhelming majority of the Oglala Sioux on this
reservation." . . .

AIM claims it was asked to the reservation by the Oglala
Sioux.

But since, at least ostensibly, the reason for the takeover
of Wounded Knee is to protest local conditions on the vast
Pine Ridge Reservation that surrounds it, a key question is
whether the takeover captures the support of the reservation's 12,000 Oglala Sioux. That support, despite the claims
of the AIM leadership, isn't altogether clear. . . .

It seems certain that the effects of the Wounded Knee
takeover will spread far beyond South Dakota. "This is going
to change history," says Mr. [Lyman] Babby [area director]
of the Bureau of Indian Affairs [an Oglala Sioux opposed
by AIM]. "The outcome will have an impact on the future
of militancy. This is the first time the Government has been
challenged in this way."

He notes that probably the last time land was seized in
the manner of Wounded Knee was the Civil War. Not since
then has a US town been taken by an armed force that tried
to set up a separate country there. He indicates the outcome
of the Wounded Knee takeover could set the stage for similar
actions on other reservations. Beyond that, it will set a prece-
dent for the US Government's response to similar tactics by
other political groups with other causes.

WOUNDED KNEE—II [4]

Here are the facts about the occupation of Wounded Knee by a group of Indians led by the American Indian Movement (AIM).

The causes leading to the current situation are these: The Oglala Sioux on the Pine Ridge Reservation have for many years complained of ill treatment by the US Government. The charges include persistent poverty, poor housing, inadequate water and health care, corruption in the Bureau of Indian Affairs, corrupt and dishonest tribal officials who are under the control of BIA superintendents, intimidation of the people, coercion to eliminate resistance, and failure of reservation economic programs due to inefficiency and dishonesty.

. . . [In 1972] the Oglalas formed a Civil Rights Organization. Failing to obtain results on specific complaints, they officially called in AIM at least three weeks before the occupation of Wounded Knee.

On Tuesday, February 27 [1973], a line of cars estimated at fifty to seventy-five, left Pine Ridge, presumably bound for Porcupine, South Dakota. Arriving at Wounded Knee, ten miles from Pine Ridge, the cars discharged their riders, who occupied the Sacred Heart Catholic Church in the town. They raided the store and trading post, taking guns and ammunition, food and supplies.

More than 80 percent of those occupying Wounded Knee are Oglala Sioux. Eleven local people were taken as "hostages." However, these must be the most peculiar hostages known in history. For, upon release, they refused to leave, and some made statements in sympathy and support of the Oglalas occupying Wounded Knee.

Federal marshals and the FBI were called in by the Bureau of Indian Affairs, "to protect the Bureau building." With them, came Department of Justice representatives,

⁴ From "Wounded Knee Seen Symbol of Resistance," by Bette Crouse Mele, staff reporter. *Wassaja* (national newspaper of Indian America). p 1+. F.-Mr. '73. Reprinted by permission.

notably Ralph Erickson and Horace Webb (a black man).
The burden of their "negotiations" was not applied to the
demands and grievances of the Oglalas, but rather to negotiating the conditions of their occupation of the building at
Wounded Knee, and the means of getting them out of there.

That the situation was considered a condition of war
was made clear by the establishment of a perimeter of Federal marshals encircling the occupied building, who moved
in huge trucks, arms, tear gas, and (according to Russell
Means, Oglala occupation leader) fifty-calibre machine
guns, a violation of the Geneva Convention. A space two
miles wide was called the DMZ (Demilitarized Zone).

Negotiations concerned the establishment of a peculiar
armed truce, with both sides promising not to shoot, and
the Federal marshals promising to maintain the encircling
perimeter, which at first was five miles from the building,
but later was judged somehow to have become not more than
two miles away.

Among the demands of the occupiers was amnesty for all
who were engaged in the action. That this was not to be
granted became clear when four Indians drove out of the
building area, and were immediately arrested. These are:
Joyce Sitting Bear, Chris Bad Eagle, Linda Statles, and Eu-
gene Hopkins. They were scheduled for arraignment on
charges of burglary, larceny, and assault on a Federal officer.
No information was given to the press as to the disposition
of the charges.

The action at Wounded Knee followed an abortive demonstration in Washington, D.C., when a Trail of Broken
Treaties caravan occupied the BIA building, leaving it damaged and records removed. A more recent action involved
hand-to-hand fighting by Indians and police at Custer, South
Dakota, when the Indians protested the killing of a Native
American youth.

Wounded Knee, it appears, is only one more step in a
spontaneous reaction to injustice. Judging from the mood

and the words of those Native Americans with whom I talked, violence will continue as long as conditions are not remedied.

There has been grievous injury to the pride of the Oglala Sioux, for the way the Government and the mass media have handled this situation. The marshals are positioned at road blocks. They point their guns directly at Indians, demanding identification and engaging in personal search.

Reporters stop people on the street at Pine Ridge, asking questions, invading privacy. Television cameras are everywhere. There is no telephone service for the people of Pine Ridge, so isolation is a fact of life. . . . When the employees of the moccasin factory at Pine Ridge came for their pay checks, the place was closed and so the people had no money for food and other expenses.

There is mixed reaction among the Oglalas themselves. Most agree that "something must be done." But many are opposed to violence. "I don't think it's necessary," said one man who refused to be identified.

An atmosphere of fear pervades this community of shacks and small houses. Fear of the tribal officers, fear of the BIA, fear of the Federal marshals, and fear of reprisals against themselves once the Wounded Knee incident is ended. . . .

The demands for redress of grievances take a twofold direction: On the one hand the Oglalas want justice established on the reservation, an end to coercion, the establishment of election procedures guaranteeing secret ballots. The other direction involves the criticisms leveled against Richard Wilson, tribal chairman.

Wilson has been accused of being the creature of the BIA, following BIA instructions, and having no regard for the rights of the people and the tribal council.

In an interview with the press, Wilson stated: "These people are bums. They are clowns and idiots. There should be no amnesty, but they should be prosecuted to the fullest extent of the law."

The conflict has been boiling since December 1972, when a newly organized group, called the Inter-District Council of the Oglala Sioux Tribe, presented charges against Wilson at the tribal council meeting, and called for his impeachment.

The action was unsuccessful, since the petitioners could not muster the necessary 15 of the 20 council members required for impeachment. Wilson, staunch foe of AIM, has thrown Dennis Banks of Minneapolis, Minnesota, off the reservation, forbidden Russell Means, AIM leader and Oglala Sioux, to hold AIM meetings on the reservation, and openly condemned AIM purposes and actions.

One result of the protest to the tribal council, and the petition to impeach the tribal chairman, was the reinstatement of tribal vice chairman David Long. He had been unilaterally removed by Wilson.

It appears to this reporter that violence will continue. The spontaneous actions being taken all over the country are proof of this. It is clear that Native Americans want justice now—not "later."

We have waited a long time, and despite small gains here and there, things are worse now than ever.

The Indian world will never be the same after Wounded Knee, it is clear. Whatever happens in that historic and tragic place, the symbol is now firmly established in the hearts and minds of the Indian people. It is a symbol of resistance when all else has failed.

A badly organized, spontaneous movement at this time, the movement for justice is bound to continue. Spontaneous and badly organized today, the organized Indian movement is yet to come. Without question alternatives to violence will be considered, but Indians will not be willing to wait, nor will they be satisfied with promises, ineffective congressional hearings, or long-drawn-out legislative proposals.

WOUNDED KNEE—III [5]

The tourists come by the hundreds every day to stare at the ruins of Wounded Knee, trying to catch some hint of the seventy-one-day-long confrontation . . . [in early 1973] between Indians and Federal marshals.

Most of the visitors seem surprised that there is so little to see. There are no bloodstains and no sign of the tens of thousands of shots that were exchanged between the Indians and the marshals from late February to early May.

A fallen roof covers the ashes of the Wounded Knee Museum, the Trading Post and the Post Office. The foundation of the destroyed church, whose picture adorns a Government antipollution poster, now looks very small. Debris has long since been cleared away.

The tourists drop beer cans into the church basement, flip cigarette butts into the wild sunflowers, tramp through the cemetery to see who is buried in a fresh grave, and then get into their cars and drive down Big Foot Trail.

Although the visible scars of the violent Wounded Knee confrontation are fading, feelings about it are still high.

On the Pine Ridge Reservation, the tribal home of the Oglala Sioux, Indian still fights Indian over whether the takeover of Wounded Knee by the American Indian Movement was a proper protest. There have been one death and several injuries since the siege ended.

The traditionalists are still in tight-lipped opposition to the movement. Many of the young Indians still support it. And both sides believe that the movement is not finished with Wounded Knee, that if it is to maintain its militancy and keep its support, it cannot be idle.

"It makes sense that AIM would pick Pine Ridge," said Judith Cornelius, who is fiercely opposed to the movement. "To be an Oglala Sioux is to be the epitome of Indianness."

[5] From "Debris of Siege at Wounded Knee Is Gone But Dispute Remains," by Martin Waldron, correspondent. New York *Times*. p 18. Ag. 9, '73. © 1973 by The New York Times Company. Reprinted by permission.

Proud, with flashing black eyes, Miss Cornelius—who is part white and part Oneida Indian—is editor of the Oglala newspaper and her slashing words are more feared by AIM than the marshals' bullets were. She is twenty-eight years old and dismisses the movement's demand as contemptuous whines for Government handouts.

While Miss Cornelius was driving with a visitor . . . through the cottonwood groves on the Pine Ridge reservation [recently], AIM leaders were seventy miles away, meditating at a sun dance.

The sun dance is one of the Indians' most sacred religious ceremonies—the strongest "medicine" of the Plains Indians.

The dance was delayed to allow AIM leaders to come to South Dakota from a national convention they held . . . in northeast Oklahoma.

The sun dance has overtones of crucifixion and maypole rites.

Until seventy-five years ago—when it was first banned by the Federal Government—the sun dance was a solemn, purification ceremony. The dancers—all male—pierced their chest muscles with animal bones or charcoal sticks and tied them to leather straps leading from a center pole. In time with throbbing drums, the dancers would prance to and fro from the center pole, leaning against the leather straps, staring at the sun, until their muscles were torn or their bones were splintered.

Sun dances were resumed sixteen years ago under an agreement with the Federal Government that only skin would be pierced. . . .

While the purification ceremony was under way, the Federal courts in South Dakota moved closer to bringing to trial the members and sympathizers of the militant movement who seized Wounded Knee. . . . A Federal judge ordered that the two most powerful men in AIM—Dennis Banks, a Chippewa Indian, and Russell Means, a Sioux—be tried together. They face eleven felony charges.

But the judge ruled that the scores of other Wounded Knee occupiers, whom the Government is determined to prosecute, would not be tried together. . . .

The Government ended the Wounded Knee standoff by agreeing to listen to the movement's complaints that the Government had not abided by treaties that it signed with the Indians in 1868.

Leonard Garment, counsel to President Nixon, was to meet . . . in Pierre, South Dakota, with "traditional chiefs and wise men" of the Sioux.

But . . . [before the date set for the meeting] Frank Fool-screw, who at seventy-six years of age is accorded the veneration that Plains Indians give their elderly, rejected the meeting place. Meet, he said, at Foolscrew's Paradise—on Indian ground. The Sioux, he said in a letter to Mr. Garment, have waited patiently since 1868 for the Government to live up to its agreements, and the Indians can wait a little longer, if necessary, so the conference can take place on Indian soil.

A SYMBOL PASSES [6]

The Dartmouth Alumni Council, the fifty-three-member "senate" representing the college's 36,000 living alumni, heard eloquent testimony [in January 1972] by Native American students at Dartmouth that continued use of the Indian symbol [at Dartmouth] represented an offensive distortion of their culture and history. Recognizing the students' concerns and also that most alumni regard the symbol as a positive depiction honoring both the Indian and Dartmouth's early history, the Council voted to establish an ad hoc "Indian Symbol Study Committee." . . . [The following is a report from the Committee's chairman, Robert D. Kilmarx.]

The first thing we were concerned about when we undertook the study of the Native Americans at Dartmouth was where the symbol came from in the first place. We found

[6] From a report of the Dartmouth Alumni Council Indian Symbol Study Committee, Robert D. Kilmarx, chairman. Bulletin (Dartmouth College). 52:1-4. Je. 30, '72. Reprinted by permission.

that a great deal of misinformation surrounds the Indian symbol. It is not, as many of us suspected, a symbol which has its roots in antiquity or in officialdom. The Indian symbol, as we know it in terms of the Indian-head profile, actually never made its appearance . . . until the early 1920s. Beyond that, it never received official recognition or sanction from anybody at the College. It just grew; it just happened.

As far as we can determine, both the symbol and the name *Indians* for the teams were results of the imagination of the Boston newspapers. Our research indicates that the first manifestation of the Indian symbol was in a Boston sports cartoon of the early 1920s depicting the now-familiar situation of a Dartmouth Indian coming down from the hills to scalp John Harvard. The Boston sportswriters picked up the concept and soon "Dartmouth Indians" was accepted as general usage.

Dartmouth, unlike Stanford University, never officially adopted the Indian symbol. Stanford's symbol originated in 1930 as a result of a specific action of their student representative body. . . . That same body [recently] repealed the 1930 action and as far as that particular organization is concerned that eliminated the Stanford Indian.

The second major project for the committee was to identify and isolate the concerns voiced and felt by the Native American students now at Dartmouth. We found that the Native Americans at Dartmouth do not feel demeaned or insulted by the Indian symbol. They don't feel outraged, but they *do* feel saddened by an inaccuracy, a grotesqueness, a hypocritical reference to a historical past. . . . This is the problem which has to be understood because the response from most people who feel strongly about the Dartmouth Indian symbol is that we aren't attempting to insult the Indians. Far from it. We look on the Indian symbol as a matter of honor, of pride, of proper recognition of a historical past; as an attribute of manliness, aggressiveness, fair-mindedness, athletic prowess and the like. How can anybody suggest to us that we are insulting or demeaning the Native Americans with those concepts. . . .

The Native Americans understand this, and therefore don't consider themselves demeaned by the symbol. But they do have, I think, three very basic, valid concerns about the symbol.

The first of these three concerns is that the Dartmouth Indian symbol represents an unreal and romantic portrayal of a past history which completely obscures a pathetic present reality. . . .

The Native Americans' number one concern, therefore, is that any idealized heroic, manly portrayal of "Indianness," such as our symbol, improperly romanticizes what is basically a most pathetic situation and represents on our part a form of moral cop-out on the responsibility to do something about it. Holding out the Dartmouth Indian symbol and proposing to honor it doesn't answer the needs which the Native Americans feel are their due from the white race. As one columnist stated, "The Indians are not expressing an outrage, they are expressing a plea for understanding of their present plight."

The second aspect of concern is that the Indian symbol is a caricature and that it leads to other more blatant caricatures. Now it's not sufficient to state "yes we understand that Indians on sweatshirts, Indians on diapers, and Indians on cocktail accouterments are improper as caricatures"—we all agree to that. Beyond that there are other more subtle caricatures, and the Indians' position is that the whole symbol is a caricature. It is a caricature because it is a white man's perception of an Indian and no white man's perception of an Indian is ever accurate. . . .

To us the Dartmouth Indian symbol is very *Indian*, but to an Indian the matters which we depict by that symbol are intimately important and sometimes sacred. Facial make-up, war-paint, facial jewelry, earrings, hairstyles, scalp locks, war bonnets, eagle feathers—to us an American artist can depict these very quickly and clearly and it says *Indian* to us. To an Indian, those things mean very significant and very subtle things, and different things depending on tribal background. As a result the Native American sees in the best aspects of our symbol basically a grotesqueness and a caricature which represents only one thing—a white man's perception of Indian, not an Indian's perception of himself. . . .

When the concerns of the Native Americans have been expressed . . . , almost invariably a sensitivity develops, an understanding develops, a sympathy develops, which results in a significant diminution in the use of the symbol. Not because anyone has ordered it, not because the College has said it shall not be, but because people have responded to a human concern. We are satisfied . . . that among those who have heard the story the attitudes have changed and changed dramatically. Those who haven't heard the story are the ones who cling to the old attitudes.

As a result, the symbol is much less in use than ever before, and that trend is continuing. It does not represent, in our view, another "giving-in" to another minority demand. There has been no demand. There has been discussion. There has been a response to the situation on the part of those most involved with it. Here are some of the specific aspects of diminution: the college itself, administratively, has not for some time used the Indian symbol on any official letterheads or any official form. The student newspaper and radio station have both editorially announced that they no longer will refer to the teams as "Indians" nor use an Indian symbol on their mastheads. The Athletic Council has made significant changes in its use of the symbol over the last several years. The Indian cheerleader has been discontinued. The Indian symbol on hockey rink equipment has been discontinued. This spring the lacrosse team revoked an earlier order of jerseys with the symbol on the sleeve and substituted an order for plain jerseys with no symbol. That wasn't because anybody told them to do it. It was because the coach and the team wanted to do it because they had come to understand the concerns of the Indian Americans and wanted to respond to them. Sports releases no longer refer to

Dartmouth Indians, the warpath, scalping, or any such white "Indianizations" and caricatures. The merchants on Main Street have informed us that they do not intend to reorder items bearing Indian-symbol imprints once current stocks are depleted. . . . The Injunaires, that renowned student singing group, no longer refer to themselves in those terms. They are the Dartmouth Aires, and that is not because they were told to do it, but because they wanted to do it. . . . Class and club newsletters have largely eliminated their caricaturizations and cartoonings of Indians; one or two remain but most have changed in response again to an understanding of the concern. . . .

We have learned a great deal in this project. We have come as individuals, and unanimously, to the conclusion that the Indian symbol is an idea whose time has gone by. It made sense at one point, but now it does not as far as we are concerned. We have heard the story and we accept it. By the same token we are not in a position, and we do not make a recommendation, to the College or to the Alumni Council, that the Indian symbol be officially discontinued. We think that this would be most inappropriate. It would be an effort to legislate attitudes in an area in which such things cannot be legislated. We are dealing with human concerns, with human attitudes, and it seems clear to us that the sorts of things that have happened to this point are the sorts of things that should continue. And if continued, they will result before very long in a complete elimination of the Indian symbol—not because it has been ordered or ordained, but because it is a human response to a human concern.

III. INDIANS AND THE FEDERAL GOVERNMENT

EDITOR'S INTRODUCTION

No minority or other special-interest group is so closely tied to the Federal Government as are the American Indians. At various times, the Government has been viewed as the battlefield enemy, the Great White Father, the guardian, the destroyer, and the protector. Central to the Government's role in dealing with the Indian has been the highly controversial Bureau of Indian Affairs. The BIA itself describes its activities in the first excerpt in this section. This is followed by more critical reports from the *New Republic* and *Christian Century*.

President Richard M. Nixon's historic 1970 message to Congress concerning Indian affairs, almost entirely ignored by Congress through 1973, follows. Senator George McGovern, the Democratic presidential candidate in 1972, sets forth his current suggestions in the fourth selection.

Another well-known scholar on Indian matters, Ernest L. Schusky, examines the somewhat contradictory status of Indians in various aspects of citizenship. A suggestion for further Federal study (for many decades, the classic reply to Indian problems) is the next selection, and, finally, there is a pro and con discussion of the continuation or abolition of the reservations.

THE BUREAU OF INDIAN AFFAIRS [1]

The Bureau of Indian Affairs is an agency of the United States Department of the Interior. The Bureau seeks to promote economic self-sufficiency for American Indians, Eski-

[1] From pamphlet entitled *Information About the Bureau of Indian Affairs*, issued by the United States Department of the Interior, Bureau of Indian Affairs. Supt. of Docs. Washington, D.C. 20402. '71. p 1-5.

mos, and Aleuts that live on or near trust lands through education and economic and community development. Approximately 488,000 of the more than 827,000 Indian and Alaska Natives in the United States lived on or near trust lands in 1971.

[Former] Commissioner of Indian Affairs Louis R. Bruce, of Sioux and Mohawk parentage, and his Indian executive team worked with Indians across the country in 1971 to help insure an organization that reflects the thinking and feelings of the majority of Indian people. They pursued five policy goals:

To transform the agency from a management to a service organization; to reaffirm the trust status of Indian land; to make the Bureau fully responsive to the Indian people it serves; to provide tribes with the option of assuming greater responsibility relating to BIA program functions; and to work with Indian organizations to become a strong advocate for all Indian interests.

They also undertook to change BIA administrative operations in order to bring about a flexible structure that could respond to Indian needs as quickly and as effectively as possible.

Since the announcement of the new goals and administrative reforms the Bureau has moved ahead in each of the policy areas. Tribes are assuming increasing responsibility for service programs formerly administered by Federal agencies.

A milestone example of tribal initiative was the Zuñi tribal involvement in all phases of BIA programs designed for the benefit of the tribe. [See "Zuñis and Jicarilla Apaches —Going Their Own Way," in Section V, below.]

Another vehicle for tribal assumption of responsibility for BIA program activities has been the so-called "Buy Indian Act" of 1910 which authorizes the Secretary of the Interior to enter into contracts with Indian tribes "for the purchase of products of Indian industry."

"Buy Indian" contracting has since evolved from procurement of needed supplies into a method for the training and employment of Indians, and finally into an instrument for greater Indian involvement into the conduct of their own affairs. . . .

As the principal Federal agency on the reservation, the Bureau works with other Federal and tribal agencies to provide a wide variety of services for Indians living on or near reservation areas. Operating in fiscal year 1971 with a budget of $361.355 million the Bureau of Indian Affairs has initiated and expanded programs to encourage economic, educational and community self-sufficiency and development. . . .

In fiscal year 1971 the Indian Action Team (IAT) program was established to provide essential training on the reservation without relocation. It includes classroom work, shop application, and on-the-job experience which enables the workers to progress toward the journeyman level of their trades. Union officials have agreed to credit trainees for the apprenticeship training received through the program.

An income of nearly $36 million for Indian tribes came from oil, gas, and mineral leases in fiscal year 1970. Indian owners received an estimated $24 million from a timber harvest of nearly 800 million board feet in fiscal year 1971.

Indian people are increasingly aware of the dollar potential of tourism. An indication of their interest in the tourist industry is shown by establishment of a number of new tribally owned motels in Indian country. An example is the $2.5 million Bottle Hollow Resort opened on the Uintah and Ouray Reservation by the Ute Tribe of Utah in the summer of 1971.

In fiscal year 1971 about 206,700 Indian children were of school age, and of these 190,200 attended school. The Bureau operated over two hundred elementary and secondary schools as well as schools in two hospitals and nineteen dormitories for Indian students attending public schools.

In keeping with the policy that the Indian community should have the right to assume responsibility for operation

of federally funded programs, four local schools were operated by all-Indian school boards under contract with the
Bureau of Indian Affairs in the 1970-71 school year. They
are Stefan High School, South Dakota; Blackwater Day
School and Rough Rock Demonstration School, Arizona;
and Ramah School, New Mexico.

All of the Bureau's elementary and secondary schools
have Indian advisory school boards which are assuming
greater responsibility for the schools' curriculum, staffing,
and educational objectives.

The English as a Second Language program is now meeting the needs of children who speak their native language
when they enter school. [See "Remodeling Indian Schools,"
by William Brandon, in Section IV, below.]

A concentrated environmental awareness program was
undertaken in Bureau of Indian Affairs schools by Bureau
educators and National Park Service personnel in the 1970-
71 school year. Almost 53,000 descendants of America's "first
environmentalists" are now involved in environmental related studies through social sciences, language arts, science,
and art curricula.

At the end of the 1970-71 school year about 2,090 students
were graduated from Bureau of Indian Affairs high schools.
Another 6,000 were graduated from public schools and 580
from mission and other private schools.

Scholarship grants provided by the Bureau and other
sources helped 10,000 Indian young people attend colleges
in 1970-71.

A post-high-school educational consortium now exists to
better meet the needs of American Indian youth in the areas
of occupational training and comprehensive general programs. The Bureau schools forming the consortium are
Haskell Indian Junior College, Southwestern Indian Poly-
technic Institute, Institute of American Indian Arts, and
Chilocco Indian School. . . .

In April 1971, 26 reservations had Bureau-funded Tribal Work Experience programs that employed 3,185 workers and benefited 12,947 people when members of the workers' families are included.

Under this program, the tribe develops work projects considered necessary to local community development. Unemployed but employable tribal members are assigned by the tribe to jobs on these projects. The Bureau of Indian Affairs turns over to the tribal officials by contract the money which would have been paid in assistance grants to these jobless workers, plus an additional $30 monthly as a work incentive. The tribe then pays each worker what he would have received in assistance, plus an additional $30. The payment is not identified as welfare.

The Bureau of Indian Affairs in 1970 contracted for an Indian Offender Rehabilitation Program to provide for Indian ex-offenders to work with potential Indian parolees in custody in Federal and state institutions. This program gives parolees a chance for gainful employment after release, and reduces the number of repeat offenders.

In the 1970 fiscal year, more than 5,000 new homes were built on Indian reservations and some 3,570 were repaired. In the next several years the Bureau anticipates approximately 7,000 to 8,000 new houses to be built each year and 3,500 units repaired yearly.

The Bureau of Indian Affairs has strengthened its role of serving the Indian people and discarded that of managing their affairs.

BIA—FRIEND OR FOE? [2]

Agitation against the BIA had been mounting over the years, and one can understand why. The Bureau is a professional bureaucracy, on the whole comparable to the British colonial service—meaning well, as Theodore Roose-

[2] From "Indians On and Off the Reservation: From Wards to Freemen," by Paul R. Wieck, contributing editor. *New Republic.* 168:16-19. Ap. 7, '73. Reprinted by permission of The New Republic, © 1973 Harrison-Blaine of New Jersey, Inc.

velt said of a fellow politician, but meaning it feebly; humane but seldom mingling with its charges after the cocktail hour, returning home after years of service loaded down with artifacts picked up from sojourns among the "natives."

I recall a friend who went to the Navajo reservation to make the first contact for VISTA. She deliberately side-stepped BIA officials, telling tribal leaders not to inform them where the meeting would be. She opened the meeting by telling the Indians it was "a historic occasion" because, for the first time in years, the Navajos were gathered to make a decision without their keepers on hand to offer guidance. The Indians were charmed; the BIA was not. But before long some revealing stories were surfacing. One VISTA volunteer serving as a schoolteacher on the Navajo reservation went to see her pupils and meet their parents in the evening and was told she was the first teacher to show enough interest in her pupils to come to their homes. That nearly a century after BIA took over the Navajo reservation.

By the late 1960s the challenge to the Bureau was out in the open. Weldell Chino, chairman of the Mescalero Apaches, took the lead as NCAI [National Congress of American Indians] president, demanding that the BIA be partially dismantled by the elimination of district offices so that a direct line of communications could be set up between the reservations (each has a BIA establishment) and the policy-makers in Washington. He criticized the Interior Committees of both branches of Congress as "land oriented" rather than "people oriented" and suggested Indian matters be moved to a special committee modeled after the "select" panel on Indian problems chaired by Senator Robert F. Kennedy (Democrat, New York) before his death and then taken over by his brother.

Chino was quite right in fingering the congressional committees as "land oriented"; time and again, the Indians have been used to promote new reclamation projects, once it became clear that almost anything could be moved through Congress if a little something for the Indians was tucked in on the side. The end result: the white man's projects, particularly in the West where most of the reservation Indians live, have appropriated much of the water and the Indians stand in real danger of ending up with a very small share of the most vital resource in that arid area of the country. It caused a minor uproar a couple of years ago when a career attorney in BIA, William Veeder, charged the Department of Interior with failing to protect Indian water rights and the Nixonians in the department tried to exile him to Phoenix. On this occasion the bulk of the tribal chairmen stood behind Veeder.

The Nixon Administration has shown a partiality for Indians who are so assimilated they are indistinguishable from the prototype of this Administration—successful, upper middle class business or professional men with a conservative life-style. It took them a while to find one as BIA commissioner. Finally they located Louis Bruce, a retired businessman. . . .

Then began a strange dance at Interior. Bruce toured the country, ingratiating himself with Indian leaders and promising almost anything, only to have Assistant Secretary of Interior Harrison Loesch, a water attorney from Colorado's western slope, say "no, no, no." Finally Loesch disassembled the staff of young activist Indians that Bruce had put together and sent a career bureaucrat with Indian lineage, John Crow, over to run BIA as Bruce's assistant. The Bureau limped along until the end of 1972 when AIM leaders led a group to Washington to occupy the BIA headquarters. In the aftermath, Loesch, Bruce and Crow were all fired. . . .

One legacy of the Bruce days at BIA, however, is the dusting off of a fairly good legislative package by the Administration, which it has presented anew in the aftermath of Wounded Knee with hints that the trouble in South Dakota might not have happened if the Congress had acted earlier. The program is popular with Indian tribal leaders and includes: elevating the BIA commissioner to assistant

secretary, so there won't be another Loesch between him
and the top man; creating a trust counsel to provide independent legal help (Indians from tribes too poor to have
their own attorneys now must rely on the Government attorneys who are often faced with a conflict-of-interest if the
Indians are quarreling with an agency like the Bureau of
Reclamation; also Indians are wary of Government attorneys
when critical matters like water rights are involved); setting
up a contracting authority to allow tribes to assume control
of BIA services funded by the Federal Government, thus
making the BIA bureaucrats employees of the tribe rather
than of the Government; and finally, new financing legislation.

It's just possible the militants at Wounded Knee have
given their political foes within the tribal structure the lev-
erage they need to force the white man to deal realistically
with Indian problems, and money in this instance isn't
everything. No one would claim Indian programs have been
generously funded, but they haven't been starved. For fiscal
year 1974 Nixon is seeking $1.45 billion (that averages out
better than $3000 per Indian and is a 15 percent jump over
F[iscal]Y[ear]73). Over the years countless billions have been
poured in, most of it to provide BIA services such as education and health care.

Congress in 1946 set up the Indian Claims Commission
with a ten-year life span to settle aboriginal land claims, a
difficult and tedious job. After twenty-five years it still hasn't
completed its work. Thus far 387 of 611 claims have been
disposed of with judgments of $490 million made to 211
claimants. The commission denied 176 claims and 224 are
still pending. The commission has put a half-billion dollars
into the reservations, some of it paid out on a per capita
basis, some retained as working capital by the tribes.

All the tribes are not as poor as the Oglala Sioux of
Wounded Knee. The Navajos, once poverty-ridden, made a
financial comeback in the post-World War II era with the
discovery of oil, uranium, helium, gas and coal under their

reservation lands and have had as much as $80-$90 million in the tribal trust fund at times, giving the nation's largest tribe (some 125,000) the resources to promote some of its own economic development. [See "Navajos—A Changing Tribe," in Section V, below.]

The key is a combination of Indian self-determination, backed up by a firm commitment by the Federal Government to protect Indians from exploitation of their natural resources and generous funding of their attempts at self-help. If Indians are not treated as Federal wards but given discriminating assistance, they can make their own way out of the isolation of a traditional and very conservative culture into a technological society, and at a pace of their own choosing. It's a course beset by all kinds of difficulties, but they're difficulties the Indians themselves understand far better than the most indulgent of their white friends. For instance, how many whites can understand the differences between the needs of the Oglala Sioux, driven from their ancestral lands and consigned to poverty, and the Pueblos whose settlements which dot the Rio Grande remain in the same place their Spanish conquerors found them late in the sixteenth century?

The biggest mistake which could be made as the Indians emerge from nearly a century of political and cultural oppression would be for the white man, no matter how well-meaning, to take it upon himself to choose sides in intra-tribal conflicts such as that at Wounded Knee.

STRUGGLE FOR LAND AND WATER [3]

As populations swell in US western cities, the need to meet increasing demands for energy is leading huge corporations—and Government agencies as well—to close in on Indian land and Indian resources. Although the United States

[3] From two-part article entitled "Indian Resources: Struggles Over Water Rights" and "Indian Resources: Development and Land Depredations," by Pat Porter, free-lance writer. *Christian Century.* 89:208-10, 225-6. F. 16-23, '72. Copyright 1972 Christian Century Foundation. Reprinted by permission from the February 16 & 23, 1972 issues of *The Christian Century.*

Department of the Interior, through its Bureau of Indian Affairs, is required by law to protect Indian interests, in fact it follows policies that continually erode the Indian economic base, particularly through the leasing of Indian natural resources to private interests.

Every Government agency has patron-client relationships with special-interest groups, both within the Government and outside it, and the Interior department is no exception. Basically a land-oriented organization, it has under its wing, among other branches, the Bureau of Reclamation, which designs and builds dams and irrigation systems, and the Bureau of Land Management, which oversees federal land. These bureaus are charged with the development of natural resources, while the Bureau of Indian Affairs acts as the Indians' trustee. In this conflict of interest situation, Interior department lawyers can often be found representing both sides of a dispute!

Urban, state and private interests coveting Indian resources are able to exert tremendous pressures on the Interior department and on congressmen. The Indians, however, as the nation's smallest and most impoverished minority group, have neither the political power nor the money required to lobby in Washington and to pursue other ways of combating the influence of these powerful interest groups, particularly when long and extremely expensive litigation is involved. . . .

The Pyramid Lake Story

. . . [A] case in which the Government has refused to help the Indians in a struggle for water rights is being pursued by six hundred Nevada Paiute Indians, who are fighting for the survival of their only economic resource: beautiful Pyramid Lake. The beginning of this usurpation of rights goes back to 1905, when the Derby dam was constructed without the knowledge or consent of the Paiutes; the dam made possible the diversion of water from the Truckee River, which feeds Pyramid Lake, to the Bureau of Reclamation's Newlands project—an outright theft.

Over the years the water thus diverted has largely gone to irrigate the area around Fallon, Nevada, to the benefit of prosperous non-Indian farmers and ranchers. Run-off water draining from the farms and grazing lands has not been returned to the river. Instead, part of it has formed marshlands, out of which have been created a public shooting ground and the Stillwater National Wildlife Refuge; the rest of it feeds an artificial lake used for recreation—a body of water less than thirty-five miles from Pyramid Lake. . . .

In a press conference . . . [in late 1971] Interior Secretary Rogers Morton pointed out that the Administration had proposed an Indian Trust Counsel Authority which would guarantee independent legal representation in land and water rights cases, but that Congress had taken no action on the proposal. As an interim measure, he said, an Indian water rights office would be created to ensure appropriate action when Indian water rights were jeopardized.

The Paiutes and the Indians of the New Mexico pueblos —and other tribes as well—are still waiting for some sign of "appropriate action" on their behalf. [On November 9, 1972, a U.S. district judge in Washington upheld the Paiute suit and ordered the Interior department to change its diversion regulations and report back to the court if Pyramid Lake failed to maintain its level.—Ed.]

As a branch of the United States Department of the Interior, the Bureau of Indian Affairs is subject to pressures to advance the interests of the Department as a whole—even when those interests violate Indian rights. The conflict of interest is not always apparent, however. Certain economic benefits to the Indians may seem to accrue from land development plans of the Bureau of Reclamation and the Bureau of Land Management—at least, the schemes may be represented in that light to tribal leaders. What the BIA has so often failed to point out to the Indians is the extent to which their land and mineral rights are being exploited, and the subsequent disastrous effects on their environment.

As an example, the Bureau of Reclamation's irrigation works on the upper Rio Grande River in New Mexico will make possible the construction of housing developments for permanent residents as well as recreational facilities and motels for vacationers—all on land belonging to the Tesuque Indian pueblo. The BIA encouraged some tribal council members to sign a ninety-nine-year lease with the Sangre de Cristo Development Company for the use of 1,300 acres of land—one third of the pueblo's total area—and a large quantity of its precious water.

The Tesuques were not informed of the lease, either by the council members who negotiated it or by the BIA—until after it was signed, and they are understandably outraged. The rent they will receive cannot begin to compensate for the prospect that their land will be alienated from them and the quality of their life changed as more and more non-Indians move into the proposed developments. And they fear that the ninety-nine-year lease eventually will mean outright loss of the land; indeed, in real estate dealings a ninety-nine-year lease is considered tantamount to a sale. . . .

And the Black Mesa

In Arizona, both the Navajo and the Hopi Indians are fighting to prevent devastation of their land and depletion of their water by a huge strip-mining operation on the Black Mesa, a semiarid plateau considered sacred by the two tribes.

The mine is being operated, under a thirty-five-year lease, by the Peabody Coal Company, the nation's largest coal producer and a subsidiary of the Kennecott Copper Company. Also located on leased Indian land are six enormous power plants which, burning coal from the Black Mesa and other nearby mines, are scheduled to provide electricity for Los Angeles, Phoenix, Las Vegas and other large cities. . . .

Faced with Interior department complicity in the exploitation of their natural resources, many Indians have questioned the position that the Bureau of Indian Affairs occupies within that Department, and some have demanded that it be moved to a more people-oriented organization, such as the Health, Education, and Welfare department. Others have suggested that the BIA be given the status of an independent agency.

A proposal advanced by the National Tribal Chairmen's Association, a recently formed organization of more than sixty-five reservation leaders, is to place the BIA in a sort of "receivership" under direct White House supervision. . . .

The Government response to the Indians' proposal to remove the BIA from the Interior department seemed evasive. Interior Secretary Rogers Morton, apparently regarding the proposal as unimportant, told the press that "it was more symbolic than actually thought out." He also spoke of the Administration's proposal for an Indian Trust Counsel Authority which would guarantee independent legal representation for land- and water-rights issues. However, it remains to be seen whether or not this agency will come into being. . . .

In the meantime, Indians of various tribes are challenging the Government by bringing to court cases involving their land and water rights. Indeed, such suits are becoming so numerous and are receiving so much attention that it is increasingly difficult for the Government to brush aside Indian interests. However, no official action has yet been taken on the fundamental problem: the conflict of interest generated while control over the Bureau of Indian Affairs is left in the hands of the Interior department—a department whose primary interest is in "developing" natural resources. Until this problem is solved, the Interior department will have the power to subvert any BIA efforts to protect Indian land and water rights.

THE PRESIDENT'S RECOMMENDATIONS [4]

The first Americans—the Indians—are the most deprived and most isolated minority group in our nation. On virtually every scale of measurement—employment, income, education, health—the condition of the Indian people ranks at the bottom.

This condition is the heritage of centuries of injustice. From the time of their first contact with European settlers, the American Indians have been oppressed and brutalized, deprived of their ancestral lands and denied the opportunity to control their own destiny. Even the Federal programs which are intended to meet their needs have frequently proven to be ineffective and demeaning.

But the story of the Indian in America is something more than the record of the white man's frequent aggression, broken agreements, intermittent remorse and prolonged failure. It is a record also of endurance, of survival, of adaptation and creativity in the face of overwhelming obstacles. It is a record of enormous contributions to this country—to its art and culture, to its strength and spirit, to its sense of history and its sense of purpose.

It is long past time that the Indian policies of the Federal Government began to recognize and build upon the capacities and insights of the Indian people. Both as a matter of justice and as a matter of enlightened social policy, we must begin to act on the basis of what the Indians themselves have long been telling us. The time has come to break decisively with the past and to create the conditions for a new era in which the Indian future is determined by Indian acts and Indian decisions.

Self-Determination Without Termination

The first and most basic question that must be answered with respect to Indian policy concerns the historic and legal

[4] From *Recommendations for Indian Policy: Message from the President of the United States Transmitting Recommendations for Indian Policy.* (House Doc. no 91-363) 91st Congress, 2d session. Supt. of Docs. Washington, D.C. 20402. '70. p 1-12.

relationship between the Federal Government and Indian communities. In the past, this relationship has oscillated between two equally harsh and unacceptable extremes.

On the one hand, it has—at various times during previous Administrations—been the stated policy objective of both the Executive and Legislative branches of the Federal Government eventually to terminate the trusteeship relationship between the Federal Government and the Indian people. As recently as August of 1953, in House Concurrent Resolution 108, the Congress declared that termination was the long-range goal of its Indian policies. This would mean that Indian tribes would eventually lose any special standing they had under Federal law: the tax-exempt status of their land would be discontinued; Federal responsibility for their economic and social well being would be repudiated; and the tribes themselves would be effectively dismantled. Tribal property would be divided among individual members who would then be assimilated into the society at large.

This policy of forced termination is wrong, in my judgment, for a number of reasons. First, the premises on which it rests are wrong. Termination implies that the Federal Government has taken on a trusteeship responsibility for Indian communities as an act of generosity toward a disadvantaged people and that it can therefore discontinue this responsibility on a unilateral basis whenever it sees fit. But the unique status of Indian tribes does not rest on any premise such as this. The special relationship between Indians and the Federal Government is the result instead of solemn obligations which have been entered into by the United States Government. Down through the years, our Government has made specific commitments to the Indian people. For their part, the Indians have often surrendered claims to vast tracts of land and have accepted life on Government reservations. In exchange, the Government has agreed to provide community services such as health, education and public safety, services which would presumably allow Indian communities to enjoy a standard of living comparable to that of other Americans.

This goal, of course, has never been achieved. But the special relationship between the Indian tribes and the Federal Government which arises from these agreements continues to carry immense moral and legal force. To terminate this relationship would be no more appropriate than to terminate the citizenship rights of any other American.

The second reason for rejecting forced termination is that the practical results have been clearly harmful in the few instances in which termination actually has been tried. [See "Should Reservations Be Abolished?" below.] The removal of Federal trusteeship responsibility has produced considerable disorientation among the affected Indians and has left them unable to relate to a myriad of Federal, state and local assistance efforts. Their economic and social condition has often been worse after termination than it was before.

The third argument I would make against forced termination concerns the effect it has had upon the overwhelming majority of tribes which still enjoy a special relationship with the Federal Government. The very threat that this relationship may someday be ended has created a great deal of apprehension among Indian groups and this apprehension, in turn, has had a blighting effect on tribal progress. Any step that might result in greater social, economic or political autonomy is regarded with suspicion by many Indians who fear that it will only bring them closer to the day when the Federal Government will disavow its responsibility and cut them adrift.

In short, the fear of one extreme policy, forced termination, has often worked to produce the opposite extreme: excessive dependence on the Federal Government. In many cases this dependence is so great that the Indian community is almost entirely run by outsiders who are responsible and responsive to Federal officials in Washington, D.C., rather than to the communities they are supposed to be serving. This is the second of the two harsh approaches which have long plagued our Indian policies. Of the Department of the Interior's programs directly serving Indians, for example, only 1.5 percent are presently under Indian control. Only 2.4 percent of HEW's [the Department of Health, Education, and Welfare] Indian health programs are run by Indians. The result is a burgeoning Federal bureaucracy, programs which are far less effective than they ought to be, and an erosion of Indian initiative and morale.

I believe that both of these policy extremes are wrong. Federal termination errs in one direction, Federal paternalism errs in the other. Only by clearly rejecting both of these extremes can we achieve a policy which truly serves the best interests of the Indian people. Self-determination among the Indian people can and must be encouraged without the threat of eventual termination. In my view, in fact, that is the only way that self-determination can effectively be fostered.

This, then, must be the goal of any new national policy toward the Indian people: to strengthen the Indian's sense of autonomy without threatening his sense of community. We must assure the Indian that he can assume control of his own life without being separated involuntarily from the tribal group. And we must make it clear that Indians can become independent of Federal control without being cut off from Federal support. My specific recommendations to the Congress are designed to carry out this policy.

1. Rejecting Termination

Because termination is morally and legally unacceptable, because it produces bad practical results, and because the mere threat of termination tends to discourage greater self-sufficiency among Indian groups, I am asking the Congress to pass a new Concurrent Resolution which would expressly renounce, repudiate and repeal the termination policy as expressed in House Concurrent Resolution 108 of the 83rd Congress. This resolution would explicitly affirm the integrity and right to continued existence of all Indian tribes and Alaska native governments, recognizing that cultural pluralism is a source of national strength. It would assure these groups that the United States Government would continue to carry out its treaty and trusteeship obligations to them as long as the groups themselves believed that such a policy was necessary or desirable. It would guarantee that whenever Indian groups decided to assume control or responsibility for Government service programs, they could do so and still receive adequate Federal financial support. In short, such a resolution would reaffirm for the Legislative branch—as I hereby affirm for the Executive branch—that the historic relationship between the Federal Government and the Indian communities cannot be abridged without the consent of the Indians.

2. *The Right to Control and Operate Federal Programs*

Even as we reject the goal of forced termination, so must we reject the suffocating pattern of paternalism. But how can we best do this? In the past, we have often assumed that because the Government is obliged to provide certain services for Indians, it therefore must administer those same services. And to get rid of Federal administration, by the same token, often meant getting rid of the whole Federal program. But there is no necessary reason for this assumption. Federal support programs for non-Indian communities—hospitals and schools are two ready examples—are ordinarily administered by local authorities. There is no reason why Indian communities should be deprived of the privilege of self-determination merely because they receive monetary support from the Federal Government. Nor should they lose Federal money because they reject Federal control. . . .

3. *Restoring the Sacred Lands Near Blue Lake*

No Government policy toward Indians can be fully effective unless there is a relationship of trust and confidence between the Federal Government and the Indian people. Such a relationship cannot be completed overnight; it is inevitably the product of a long series of words and actions. But we can contribute significantly to such a relationship by responding to just grievances which are especially important to the Indian people.

Once such grievance concerns the sacred Indian lands at and near Blue Lake in New Mexico. From the fourteenth century, the Taos Pueblo Indians used these areas for religious and tribal purposes. In 1906, however, the United States Government appropriated these lands for the creation of a national forest. According to a recent determination of the Indian Claims Commission, the Government "took said lands from petitioner without compensation."

For sixty-four years, the Taos pueblo has been trying to regain possession of this sacred lake and watershed area in order to preserve it in its natural condition and limit its non-Indian use. The Taos Indians consider such action essential to the protection and expression of their religious faith.

The restoration of the Blue Lake lands to the Taos Pueblo Indians is an issue of unique and critical importance to Indians throughout the country. I therefore take this opportunity wholeheartedly to endorse legislation which would restore 48,000 acres of sacred land to the Taos Pueblo people, with the statutory promise that they would be able to use these lands for traditional purposes and that except for such uses the lands would remain forever wild. [This has since been accomplished.—Ed.] . . .

4. *Indian Education*

One of the saddest aspects of Indian life in the United States is the low quality of Indian education. Drop-out rates for Indians are twice the national average and the average educational level for all Indians under Federal supervision is less than six school years. Again, at least a part of the problem stems from the fact that the Federal Government is trying to do for Indians what many Indians could do better for themselves.

The Federal Government now has responsibility for some 221,000 Indian children of school age. While over 50,000 of these children attend schools which are operated directly by the Bureau of Indian Affairs, only 750 Indian children are enrolled in schools where the responsibility for education has been contracted by the BIA to Indian school boards. Fortunately, this condition is beginning to change. The Ramah Navajo Community of New Mexico and the Rough Rock and Black Water Schools in Arizona are notable examples of schools which have recently been brought under local Indian control. Several other communities are now negotiating for similar arrangements.

Consistent with our policy that the Indian community should have the right to take over the control and operation of federally funded programs, we believe every Indian community wishing to do so should be able to control its own Indian schools. This control would be exercised by school boards selected by Indians and functioning much like other school boards throughout the nation. . . .

5. *Economic Development Legislation*

Economic deprivation is among the most serious of Indian problems. Unemployment among Indians is ten times the national average; the unemployment rate runs as high as 80 percent on some of the poorest reservations. Eighty percent of reservation Indians have an income which falls below the poverty line; the average annual income for such families is only $1,500. As I said in September of 1968, it is critically important that the Federal Government support and encourage efforts which help Indians develop their own economic infrastructure. To that end, I am proposing the "Indian Financing Act of 1970."

This act would do two things:

1. It would broaden the existing Revolving Loan Fund, which loans money for Indian economic development projects. I am asking that the authorization for this fund be increased from approximately $25 million to $75 million.

2. It would provide additional incentives in the form of loan guarantees, loan insurance and interest subsidies to encourage *private* lenders to loan more money for Indian economic projects. An aggregate amount of $200 million would be authorized for loan guarantee and loan insurance purposes.

I also urge that legislation be enacted which would permit any tribe which chooses to do so to enter into leases of its land for up to ninety-nine years. Indian people now own over 50 million acres of land that are held in trust by the Federal Government. In order to compete in attracting investment capital for commercial, industrial and recreational development of these lands, it is essential that the tribes be able to offer long-term leases. Long-term leasing is preferable to selling such property since it enables tribes to preserve the trust ownership of their reservation homelands. But existing law limits the length of time for which many tribes can enter into such leases. Moreover, when long-term leasing is allowed, it has been granted by Congress on a case-by-case basis, a policy which again reflects a deep-rooted pattern of paternalism. The twenty reservations which have already been given authority for long-term leasing have realized important benefits from that privilege and this opportunity should now be extended to all Indian tribes. . . .

6. *More Money for Indian Health*

Despite significant improvements in the past decade and a half, the health of Indian people still lags twenty to twenty-five years behind that of the general population. The average age at death among Indians is forty-four years, about one third less than the national average. Infant mortality is nearly 50 percent higher for Indians and Alaska natives than for the population at large; the tuberculosis rate is eight times as high and the suicide rate is twice that of the general population. Many infectious diseases such as trachoma and dysentery that have all but disappeared among other Americans continue to afflict the Indian people.

This Administration is determined that the health status of the first Americans will be improved. In order to initiate expanded efforts in this area, I will request the allocation of an additional $10 million for Indian health programs for the current fiscal year. This strengthened Federal effort will enable us to address ourselves more effectively to those problems which are particularly important to the Indian community. We understand, for example, that areas of greatest concern to Indians include the prevention and control of alcoholism, the promotion of mental health and the control of middle-ear disease. We hope that the ravages of middle-ear disease—a particularly acute disease among Indians—can be brought under control within five years.

These and other Indian health programs will be most effective if more Indians are involved in running them. Yet —almost unbelievably—we are presently able to identify in this country only thirty physicians and fewer than four hundred nurses of Indian descent. To meet this situation, we will expand our efforts to train Indians for health careers.

7. *Helping Urban Indians*
  . . . Some authorities even estimate that more Indians are living in cities and towns than are remaining on the reservation. Of those American Indians who are now dwelling in urban areas, approximately three fourths are living in poverty.

The Bureau of Indian Affairs is organized to serve the 462,000 reservation Indians. The BIA's responsibility does not extend to Indians who have left the reservation, but this point is not always clearly understood. As a result of this misconception, Indians living in urban areas have often lost out on the opportunity to participate in other programs designed for disadvantaged groups. As a first step toward helping the urban Indians, I am instructing appropriate officials to do all they can to ensure that this misunderstanding is corrected. . . .

8. *Indian Trust Counsel Authority*

The United States Government acts as a legal trustee for the land and water rights of American Indians. These rights are often of critical economic importance to the Indian people; frequently they are also the subject of extensive legal dispute. In many of these legal confrontations, the Federal Government is faced with an inherent conflict of interest. The Secretary of the Interior and the Attorney General must at the same time advance *both* the *national* interest in the use of land and water rights *and* the *private* interests of Indians in land which the Government holds as trustee.

Every trustee has a legal obligation to advance the interests of the beneficiaries of the trust without reservation and with the highest degree of diligence and skill. Under present conditions, it is often difficult for the Department of the Interior and the Department of Justice to fulfill this obligation. No self-respecting law firm would ever allow itself to represent two opposing clients in one dispute; yet the Federal Government has frequently found itself in precisely that position. There is considerable evidence that the Indians are the losers when such situations arise. More than that, the credibility of the Federal Government is damaged whenever it appears that such a conflict of interest exists.

In order to correct this situation, I am calling on the Congress to establish an Indian Trust Counsel Authority to assure independent legal representation for the Indians' natural resource rights. . . .

9. *Assistant Secretary for Indian and Territorial Affairs*

To help guide the implementation of a new national policy concerning American Indians, I am recommending to the Congress the establishment of a new position in the Department of the Interior—Assistant Secretary for Indian and Territorial Affairs. At present, the Commissioner of Indian Affairs reports to the Secretary of the Interior through the Assistant Secretary for Public Land Management—an officer who has many responsibilities in the natural resources area which compete with his concern for Indians. A new Assistant Secretary for Indian and Territorial Affairs would have only one concern—the Indian and territorial peoples, their land, and their progress and well-being. . . .

The Indians of America need Federal assistance—this much has long been clear. What has not always been clear, however, is that the Federal Government needs Indian energies and Indian leadership if its assistance is to be effective in improving the conditions of Indian life. It is a new and balanced relationship between the United States Government and the first Americans that is at the heart of our approach to Indian problems. And that is why we now approach these problems with new confidence that they will successfully be overcome.

A PROGRAM FOR JOBS [5]

The time has long since passed for the Congress and indeed for the country as a whole to come to grips with the current living conditions on the Indian reservations of this country.

It is impossible to turn back the clock, no matter how justified that action would be. It is not realistic to attempt to return to the terms of the Sioux Treaty of 1868, nor do I believe that a majority of the Indian people would desire that. It is important, however, for us to initiate a policy that will provide greater opportunities for our Indian citizens.

It is inexcusable that a visitor from the Brookings Institution to the reservations in the year 1971 would have to describe his observations as follows:

An Indian reservation can be characterized as an open-air slum. It has a feeling of emptiness and isolation. There are miles and miles of dirt or gravel roads without any signs of human life. The scattered Indian communities are made up of scores of tarpaper shacks or log cabins with one tiny window and a stovepipe sticking out of a roof that is weighted down with pieces of metal

[5] From "The Indian Economic Development and Employment Act of 1973," by Senator George McGovern (Democrat, South Dakota). *Congressional Record* (93d Congress, 1st session). 119:S11414-16. Je. 19, '73.

and automobile tires. These dwellings, each of them home for six or seven persons, often have no electricity or running water—sometimes not even an outhouse. The front yards are frequently littered with abandoned, broken-down automobiles that are too expensive to repair and too much trouble to junk. The number of unemployed is striking. Everywhere there seem to be dozens of Indians standing around doing nothing.

We must guarantee that a visitor to the reservations in the year 1981 would not be able to relate that observation.

On April 9 . . . [1973], Mr. Lloyd Eagle Bull, the secretary of the Oglala Sioux Tribal Council in South Dakota, concluded his statement before the House Subcommittee on Indian Affairs by saying:

> And now we have gotten to the real issue. The issue isn't Wounded Knee. It isn't the treaty of 1868. The issue is jobs. . . . I want to tell you that there is nothing more important that you can do for my people than to get a job program for us. We have an unemployment problem which goes back for generations. No wonder that so many people, even young people, lose hope. Get us jobs, and there won't be an Indian problem anymore.

I fully believe that Mr. Eagle Bull is right. The root cause of the problems of Indian health, social stability, and educational incentive seems clearly to be economic deprivation. The high rate of self-destruction among Indians in the twenty to thirty-four age group, that group which in our society is one of the most productive, has been attributed by Dr. Emery A. Johnson, the director of the Indian Health Service, to the total frustration, the sense of hopelessness, which stems from the lack of opportunities on the reservation.

Indian people should not have to leave the reservation —their friends, relatives, customs, and past, to participate along with the rest of the country in the most affluent society in the history of man. We in the Congress formed the reservation boundaries, and now it is our duty and responsibility to try as best we can to bring to the reservation the opportunities we have brought to the other parts of the country. We must make an affirmative and substantial commitment to Indian development; our goal must be to give the Indian people the opportunity for economic parity with other Americans.

Perhaps we have already forgotten the effects of the Great Depression [of the 1930s] on our country: the humility of being unemployed, the feelings of inadequacy when one could not provide food for his family, the frustration of having no control over one's destiny. Yet at the depth of the depression the rate of male unemployment reached only 25 percent. The Indian reservations of this country have for decades had to endure a rate of unemployment almost double that figure, and even today the rate of unemployment on the Crow Creek Reservation, for example, in my own state of South Dakota is a staggering 70 percent of the labor force.

It was clear in the 1930s that only the Federal Government had the resources and capabilities to prime the pump and break the unemployment cycle. It is equally clear to me today that the Federal Government is again uniquely capable of effectively acting to remedy the present situation.

Although in the . . . [1972-73] fiscal year over $900 million will reach the reservations from the various Federal agencies, this amount simply provides for the public services that would otherwise be funded by state and local governments. What is needed is what was called for by the Interior department Task Force appointed by Secretary Udall in 1961 [Stewart Lee Udall, Secretary of the Interior, 1961-1969] and by the report of the President's Task Force on Indian Affairs in 1967: a combined on-the-job training and public works program to provide immediate employment on Indian reservations and to upgrade the skills of the many unskilled unemployed.

Indian leaders to whom I have spoken are practically unanimous in their feeling that work programs such as those initiated by the Civilian Conservation Corps in the 1930s, the public works acceleration program in the early 1960s, and by the Emergency Employment Act of 1971 were enormously popular and successful.

It is for these reasons . . . that I am today introducing on behalf of myself and my colleague . . . [Senator Henry M. Jackson (Democrat, Washington)] the Indian Economic Development and Employment Act of 1973.

The Bureau of Indian Affairs reports that there are approximately sixty thousand reservation Indians unemployed, for a 40 percent rate of unemployment, with substantial numbers of other persons underemployed. It is my hope that the legislation which we are introducing today will reduce by one third the rate of unemployment, providing twenty thousand jobs on reservations across the country with concomitant increases in security and stability for the entire community. In addition, the multiplier effect of the infusion of purchasing power into the area will likely lead to the creation of other jobs in the now small private sectors of the reservations.

The program itself is to be administered by the Secretary of Labor, with the applicant tribes submitting their applications to the Secretary for approval. Any tribe, on Federal or state reservation, where the rate of unemployment is equal to or greater than 18 percent of the labor force, is eligible to formulate its own public-service job program and apply to the Secretary for funding.

The widest possible discretion is to be allowed the applicant in the formulation of its plans so that the tribe might set its own priorities as to what public-service projects would be most beneficial to the reservation. Some guidelines are of course prescribed, and the plan must provide for the employment of at least 20 percent of those unemployed. But generally a philosophy of self-determination is to be encouraged. All projects are to be located within the geographical area over which the applicant tribe exercises political jurisdiction; and all employees are to be Indians, except where it is advisable to hire outside supervisory personnel with special expertise. Indian culture and identity should be respected and preserved. . . .

At the same time, . . . I think we must once again address the overall goals with respect to American Indian reservations.

Since 1953, under House Concurrent Resolution 108 of that session, we have pursued the course of termination. Our efforts have been designed to integrate the American Indian into white society in every respect, and to terminate the special relationship that has existed between the Government and the reservations. Over time it was expected to end the reservation system.

That policy has been a disaster, for reservation and non-reservation Indians alike. Eliminating the reservations cannot eliminate the Indian problem; instead it is aggravated. For those who have little else, the policy takes away their identity and their roots as well.

Therefore, I am also submitting a concurrent resolution, similar to one I have sponsored before, to repeal the 1953 resolution. It is time to put aside the fears and the false impressions the termination policy has fostered, and to declare our intention that the Indian people will be permitted to retain their rich cultural heritage and choose their own destiny.

CIVIL RIGHTS DILEMMA [6]

The dilemma facing Indians in the United States today is to choose between their rights as tribal members and their civil liberties as US citizens. On the one hand tribal law guarantees special privileges; on the other it deprives Indians of constitutional protection in due process, education and religion. Although the dilemma is long standing, an analysis of it has begun only recently. A notable expression

[6] From "An Indian Dilemma," by Ernest L. Schusky, professor of anthropology, Southern Illinois University. *International Journal of Comparative Sociology*. 11:58-66. Mr. '70. Reprinted by permission.

of the dilemma is seen in the 1961 American Indian Chicago Conference; President Kennedy's Task Force on Indian Affairs further documented it; hearings before a subcommittee of the Senate Judiciary Committee also illustrate the dilemma.

These sources, as well as others, reveal a pattern in which the rights of Indians as tribal members conflict with their rights as citizens. The background for this conflict arises from governmental policy formulated piece-meal through treaties, Acts of Congress, United States Supreme Court decisions and executive action....

Due Process

A striking denial of civil liberties occurs in many tribal courts where legal counsel is not only unavailable but prohibited. Until recently, attorneys were not allowed even in the Courts of Indian Offenses which were established by the Secretary of the Interior. Although a US district court has declared this practice unconstitutional, most tribal constitutions or bylaws still have rules prohibiting attorneys. Therefore, the individual Indian's right as a US citizen to counsel and due process may still be violated.

This practice is only one of many which makes an Indian court unique. Indian communities have one of three types of courts. There are fifty-three tribal courts established by constitutions or ordinances under the Indian Reorganization Act; twelve Courts of Indian Offenses created by the administrative authority of the Secretary of the Interior; and nineteen traditional courts among the Pueblo Indians of New Mexico.

The tribal courts are modeled after the Courts of Indian Offenses. The Subcommittee on Constitutional Rights found "little resemblance" between either of these types of courts and those of the state or Federal government. The Subcommittee noted that a trial by jury may be possible only when a judge finds a substantial question of fact involved. Then, as few as six persons serve on the jury; only three of the jurors selected from the venire may be challenged; and the verdict is decided by majority vote. No provision is made for a grand jury. Moreover, on some Indian reservations there is no right of appeal; on others, the original judge may sit with a panel of judges in the appellate court. A number of tribes have only one judge, even though provision may be made for a panel; in these instances, the subcommittee also found him sitting as the sole appeal judge. The Subcommittee concluded that legislation is necessary to clarify the extent to which constitutional rights are limited by tribal authority. . . .

Indian Lands

Another issue involving Indian rights is land ownership. On the one hand a technical problem has grown out of inherited trust land. Multiple heirs hold an undivided interest in such land, and compensation for its use or purchase is diffcult. For instance, when a 116-acre tract on the Crow Creek Reservation was condemned for the Fort Randall Dam, ninety-nine heirs filed claims.

On the other hand, the trust status is a symbol of the Indian's special tie to the Government because it represents the Federal Government's obligation to provide such services as health and education. Furthermore, the reservation symbolizes a feeling that can only be termed "Indianness." Many Indians strongly feel that their land is vital for preservation of their culture and identity. Therefore, the reservation is more than a home; it is a vital part of the community's identity as *Indian*.

The importance of special rights to land is illustrated by a corresponding privilege. Recently, Indians have argued strongly for their exclusion from state game rules on the reservation, where they generally ignore state hunting or fishing regulations. Protests such as "fish-ins" have clearly been demonstrations to show the possession of special rights. Exclusion from state rules is, like land, symbolic of a community being Indian.

Unlike game rights, however, special ownership of land underlies much of the Indian dilemma. Although the Supreme Court has ruled that the trust nature of property is compatible with US citizenship, the special status clearly sets limits on citizens' rights. In particular, the trust status has led to the Federal Government's provision of other services, again affecting civil rights. Although basic problems are created by trust provisions, the termination of trusteeship is no solution. Much Indian land would be lost and state governments would replace the Federal Government. Both events are seen by Indians as a serious threat. . . .

Religion

Mission churches on reservations parallel schools in problems of responsibility. National boards of missions finance Indian churches and do not allow the local control that a nonmission church has. Similarly, participation and involvement in the Indian church are minimal. Thus, churches resemble schools, and national missions are in a position much like the Bureau of Indian Affairs. Of course, civil rights are not involved, but Indians could be learning more responsibility in their churches as preparation to assume controls elsewhere. If missions could find some means of delegating major responsibility to local churches while still financing them, a model for the Federal Government would be provided.

However, the major civil rights issue in regard to religion is the use of peyote by the Native American Church. Before 1930, many "pagan" practices were prohibited, but since then there has been little interference with Indian religious [practices] except for the Native American Church. Opposition is overtly based on the fact that peyote produces unknown biological effects and possibly affects health, but some opponents simply seem intolerant of different ritual and belief.

Whatever the basis of the opposition, an important question of civil liberty is involved. Many states outlawed use or possession of peyote although Federal laws do not include it as a narcotic. Even if it were a narcotic, the question remains: Can a religious custom be prohibited by the state? The California State Supreme Court held that religious *practices*, but not *beliefs*, may be abridged under the First Amendment. . . .

However, other state courts have interpreted as unconstitutional the prohibition of peyote within the church. For example, a California district court recently ruled that the legislature could not ban a peyote sacrament, and a superior county court in Arizona rendered a similar judgment. According to the latter decision, ". . . the practical effect of the statute outlawing (peyote's) use is to prevent worship by members of the Native American Church. . . . The manner in which peyote is used by the Indian worshipper is not inconsistent with the public health, morals, or welfare."

WHITE HOUSE CONFERENCE [7]

To find a workable solution to the problems and to begin to grant justice to the First Americans, it is strongly recommended by many Indian leaders and groups that the President immediately call an emergency National Conference on American Indians, which could be patterned after previous successful White House conferences. There will be many obstacles to such a conference, such as racism, apathy, ignorance, bureaucratic red tape, and professional ineptitude, but this should not deter the conference from searching for answers to the red man's dilemma.

One major difference from past efforts, and a vital factor in the success of such a proposed conference, would be its comprehensiveness and the direct involvement of Indians at all levels, both in the conference itself and in the implementation of recommendations that come out of it. There has never been such an all-Indian conference on a national level.

[7] From "A White House Conference on the American Indian," by Charles E. Farris, a Cherokee; assistant professor, School of Social Work, Barry College, Miami Shores, Florida. *Social Work*. 18:80-6. Ja. '73. Reprinted with permission of the author and the National Association of Social Workers.

The conference could logically develop from and utilize the established mechanism of the 1970-71 regional hearings conducted by ... [Vice-President Agnew's] National Council on Indian Opportunity. To provide equitable representation, each legally recognized Indian tribe would, under the supervision of a national Indian organization such as the National Congress of American Indians, elect a proportionate number of tribal representatives, based on the latest US census tabulations of those confirmed tribal members aged eighteen years and over. A ratio of one representative to each one thousand Indians from each tribe might be considered. The total number of representatives for each tribe could be divided proportionately between reservation and nonreservation Indians. To counterbalance the influence of the larger tribal groups, there would be an additional at-large delegate from each tribe, irrespective of the tribe's size.

Policy decisions would be determined by a two-thirds vote. The Federal Government would pay all the conference expenses, so there would be no financial hardship to inhibit tribal participation. To provide continuity, provisions would be made for a follow-up conference mechanism, e.g., standing committees to conduct independent studies and funnel recommendations to the tribes for appropriate action.

Bureau of Indian Affairs

The policies, internal reorganization, and administrative repositioning of the Bureau of Indian Affairs (BIA) should be the first order of business. Historically the primary responsibility of BIA has been "the management, conservation and development of the nation's water, fish, wildlife, mineral, forest, and park and recreational resources." Its purposes state almost as an afterthought that "it also has major responsibilities for Indian and Territorial Affairs."

Even with BIA's alleged weakness and negative history, one should exercise caution in recommending modification of BIA's contractual relationship with the Indian. Many Indians prefer the familiarity of BIA, even with its problems, to some of the proposed substitutes. In many circles it is felt that BIA deserves no censure because it has been and continues to be merely the instrument through which the Federal Government's anti-Indian policies have been carried out. The truth is, that if BIA had not had many dedicated and concerned employees, the Indian might well have been exterminated.

BIA has long been inadequately funded and improperly staffed. For example, in 1969 BIA's total budget was approximately $500 million, of which $290 million was for the Indians; the ratio of staff to reservation Indians was one to eighteen. Thus the major concerns of the conference should be as follows: (1) Should BIA's major responsibility be shifted from land conservation to Indian affairs? (2) How should such a change be implemented? (3) What role should BIA assume in relation to the nonreservation Indian?

The Indian tribes have never been involved in a significant or meaningful way in the development of programs for the Indian. It is essential that any program reform should directly involve the Indian tribal groups and reflect tribal thinking and planning. For too long there have been too many bureaucratic chiefs and not enough blanket Indians involved in policy making. In addition, program planners have ignored the diversity and heterogeneity of the more than three hundred distinct Indian tribal cultures. One general Indian policy, regardless of how well intentioned or conceived, cannot be applied equally to so many different cultures. Unless the programs are compatible with Indian tribal life, they are doomed to failure.

Another cornerstone for a new Indian program should be a recognition of and respect for the uniqueness of the individual Indian; past programs have failed to do so. The Indian has always had a special concern and respect for each person's right to live his own life without outside interference as long as he does not hurt his fellow man. For example, an Indian prayer to the Great Spirit says: "Before being critical of one's neighbor, one should walk a mile in the neighbor's moccasins." This philosophy is further reflected in the Indian's natural reluctance to be competitive or aggressive in personal relationships. He has always stood ready to give assistance to and share with his needy fellow men. Ironically, the early American settlers' survival depended on the help freely offered by the American Indian.

Programs should also be sensitive to the red man's deep reverence for nature and land, which is the central theme of many of the tribal religions. [Scott] Momaday, the only American Indian to win the Pulitzer prize, captures this reverence eloquently:

There was a house made of dawn. It was made of pollen and rain, and the land was very old and everlasting. There were many colors on the hills, and the plain was bright with different-colored clays and sands. Red and blue and spotted horses grazed in the plain, and there was a dark wilderness on the mountains beyond. The land was still and strong. It was beautiful all around.

The Indian's very survival required that his life-style be compatible and harmonious with nature, and this was related to his worship.

For examination purposes, the problems currently facing the red man may be divided into three major areas: economics, education, and health. . . .

Economics

Today a new economic base must be designed for the red man. The reservation Indian needs constructive help in developing broad economic programs to sever his dependence on reservation lands. But more important, there is a limit to the number of Indians who can support themselves adequately by farming on the reservation. To create a viable economy, the Indian needs programs of technical assistance so he can develop his own technological and economic expertise and competence in farming, ranching, mining, tourism, fishing, lumbering, industry, ecology, and so forth.

Adequate financial aid, such as short-term low-interest revolving loans or direct grants, should be readily available to reservation and nonreservation Indians, or co-op groups should be formed. Financial assistance should not be restricted to the Indian's own money, obtained from the involuntary sale of his lands, that has been held in trust by Federal agencies and usually requires time-consuming BIA approval for release.

The Indian should have freedom and assistance to live in an environment that provides the optimum conditions for social and economic growth. He should not be forced off the reservation and into complete assimilation just so he can lead a decent life. This means that the reservation must provide the economic security necessary so that the Indian does not have to leave it.

Education

Indian and non-Indian educators agree that there is a need for major revisions in Indian education programs. [See articles in Section IV, below.] What type of revision and how much are the unanswered questions. The author puts forth the following issues that could be considered by Indians at the proposed White House Conference:

1. A National Board of Indian Education should be established, with authority to set minimum national standards for Indian education and to do in-depth studies of both on- and off-reservation Indian education programs. Groups such as the National Indian Education Association could provide valuable consultation.

2. More Indian teachers are necessary. What should their training consist of and how should they be utilized?

3. Most Indian students need financial help to continue their education. How can more college scholarships be developed for them?

4. In 1968 six thousand Indian children were not enrolled in school. Why are so many children not attending school? Why is the dropout rate twice as high for Indians as is the national average? What can be done about these problems?

5. How can there be more responsible participation by Indian parents in the education of their children?

6. Because there is a shortage of schools on the reservations, most Indian children must be sent to boarding schools if they are to be educated. How can adequate funds be obtained to build and operate enough schools on the reservation so that children do not have to live away from home?

7. If sufficient on-reservation schools are built, there will be no need for boarding schools. These buildings then could be converted into other facilities, such as centers for treating emotionally disturbed children or nursing homes. What is the best use that can be made of these facilities?

8. Because of the poor education Indian children now receive and the deprivation they experience, programs must be instituted to individualize instruction and provide tutorial assistance to help these children catch up. To accomplish this goal, preschool programs must be implemented that utilize experts in early childhood education. Also bilingual programs must be developed with the help of experts in linguistics.

9. High unemployment and unskilled labor are characteristic of reservation Indians. On- and off-reservation vocational training programs must be instituted to help adult Indians become competitive in the marketplace.

10. Money earmarked for Indian education must be policed so that it is spent only for this purpose.

Health

The improvement of Indian health is vital. Although the United States Public Health Service is to be commended for the many improvements it has made in Indian health services since it took over this responsibility in 1956, there are many serious health problems still needing attention. The White House Conference might address itself to the following health questions:

1. Why does the Indian live an average of only forty-four years?

2. Why is the mortality rate for infants aged one month and over three times the national average?

3. Why is the suicide rate among Indian teen-agers five times the national average?

4. How can sufficient well-staffed hospitals and clinics, easily accessible to all Indians, be provided?

5. How can emotional illness and alcoholism be combated among Indians?

6. Why are there recruitment problems in obtaining professional personnel for Indian health programs?

7. How can effective public health education programs be developed among the Indians?

8. How can Indians cope with ecological problems on the reservation?

9. What can be done about substandard housing both on and off the reservations?

Conclusions

It is obvious that Federal policies and programs regarding the Indian are urgently in need of change. As a first step, the President should call a White House Conference on American Indians that would be financed by the Federal Government. This national conference should have a structure that would provide equitable representation for all Indians, both reservation and nonreservation. Social workers and other professionals should be actively involved in this conference, but they should not relegate the Indian to second place in solving his own problems. Thus there must be Indian participation and control at all levels. For the proper and prompt implementation of any recommended program changes, adequate financial support, with appropriate legislative and administrative rulings, will be essential. It is also important that there be a built-in ongoing evaluation mechanism by which the Indians can take corrective action when indicated.

SHOULD RESERVATIONS BE ABOLISHED [8]

Keep the Reservation System as It Is

For many Indians, the land they hold is sacred. Sometimes certain plots of land have religious significance for Indian tribes. In other cases, tribes value the land simply because it is theirs.

"The reservations are all that remain of the continent the Indians once owned, and they are determined to fight for every handful of dust that remains," says Vine Deloria, Jr., a Standing Rock Sioux and author of *Custer Died for Your Sins*.

"Termination," *Time* magazine reports, "is now heatedly rejected by nearly all Indian leaders." Instead of blending into the cities and towns of non-Indian America, most Indians prefer to emphasize their own distinctive heritage and culture, and they feel they can do this best by remaining on their own lands. Many Indians today are not so sure they want to be assimilated into the mainstream of modern American life.

Even if termination were a good thing for some tribes, supporters of the present system argue, it might not be good for all. Indian tribes differ so much that their termination experiences would be widely different. For example, some tribes may be economically sound enough to stand on their own, but others are not. After the 1961 termination of the Menominee reservation, the Wisconsin state government paid out more than six times as much money in welfare to the tribe as it had before termination. Some businesses on the reservation were prospering before termination, but were unsuccessful after the reservation closed.

The most obscene word you can say to an Indian leader [according to David R. Maxey of *Look* magazine] is *termination*. . . . This policy was last tried in the Eisenhower years under the leadership of Senator Arthur Watkins [Republican] of Utah. He used

[8] From article "Indian Reservations: Should They Be Abolished?" *Senior Scholastic.* 97:21-3. S. 28, '70. Reprinted by permission from *Senior Scholastic,* © 1970 by Scholastic Magazines, Inc.

the rhetoric of "giving Indians first-class citizenship." Watkins hustled several relatively wealthy tribes onto the terminated list, which soon left them headed for . . . the white folks' welfare rolls.

The most important reason why Indian reservations should be maintained, supporters argue, is that the United States is under solemn treaty obligations to keep the reservations intact. "Never did the United States give any Indian tribe any land at all," says Vine Deloria, Jr., "Rather, the Indian tribes gave the United States land in consideration for having Indian title to the remaining land confirmed." . . .

Terminate All Indian Reservations

"By our Government policy we have tried to destroy the pride and culture and customs of Indians," says Senator Fred Harris (Democrat, Oklahoma) whose wife is part Comanche Indian. There is no guarantee that Indian culture would flourish if reservations were terminated, and if Indians were to join the American "mainstream." But it has certainly not flourished under reservation conditions.

Reservation schools are poor by the educational standards of the rest of the nation. For years they were staffed mostly by white instructors who made Indian children feel as though they should be ashamed of their cultural heritage. "We're always downgraded because we're Indian," said one eighteen-year-old Indian high school student on the Blackfoot Indian Reservation in Montana. "The popular culture is always telling us that Indians are dirty and shiftless, and we tend to see ourselves as others see us."

Termination is hardly a cure-all, but its advocates argue that it can go a long way in giving an Indian community the self-confidence it needs to participate more fully in society. Many Menominee Indians are pleased with the termination experiment, now ten years old, of their Wisconsin reservation. James Frechette—chairman of the trust corporation which operates Menominee land resources—admits that reservation Indians elsewhere believe that the Menominee termination has not been a success. But, he adds, "I don't believe it. I for one would not go back to the old system." And Richard R. Dodge, another Menominee Indian, states proudly: "We have thrown off the yoke of dependency."

Throughout US history the reservation system and its "yoke of dependency" have tried to make Indians conform to white institutions instead of allowing them the right of choosing their own life style. Today the Menominees are a rare exception in a nation of Indians highly dependent on the Federal Government for employment, shelter, and in some cases even food and clothing.

Such a serious condition cannot be corrected merely by changing the Bureau of Indian Affairs, critics say. It is time to end the entire paternalistic and stifling reservation system and let the Indians move freely into society as *complete* Americans.

IV. EDUCATION—VITAL INGREDIENT

EDITOR'S INTRODUCTION

Indian and white groups agree that the improvement and expansion of education of Indian children and youth can be the key ingredient in solving many of the problems discussed elsewhere in this volume. Both the progress in education, and the lack of it, are reviewed in this section. Dr. Wilcomb E. Washburn, historian, author, and chairman of the department of American studies at the Smithsonian Institution, and Richard Margolis, author and poet, present the general picture. Promising aspects of higher education are found in the third selection, from *Newsweek*. What, then, are the options? William Brandon, another free-lance writer, has suggestions in the final article.

THE STATUS TODAY [1]

In 1969 there were 178,476 Indian students, ages five to eighteen, enrolled in public, Federal, private and mission schools. Approximately 12,000 children of this age group were not in school. Of the total in school, 119,000 were in public schools, 36,263 in boarding schools operated by the Bureau of Indian Affairs, 16,100 in Bureau day schools, 108 in Bureau hospital schools, and 4,089 in dormitories maintained by the Bureau for children attending public schools. The Bureau operated 77 boarding schools, 144 day schools, 2 hospital schools and 18 dormitories. The number of Indian children being educated in public schools has steadily

[1] Excerpts from *Red Man's Land/White Man's Law*, by Wilcomb E. Washburn, chairman, department of American studies, Smithsonian Institution. Scribner, '71. p 224-6. Reprinted with the permission of Charles Scribner's Sons. Copyright © 1971 Wilcomb E. Washburn.

increased, aided by the financial assistance provided local
school districts under the Johnson-O'Malley Act of 1934
(which provides financial support to fourteen states and four
separate school districts with large Indian populations) and
under Public Law 874 (which provided financial support,
in cooperation with the Department of Health, Education,
and Welfare, to aid federally affected areas). The closer
relationship between state school systems and the Indian
system has been welcomed by many Indian groups. Sixty-one
tribes have established compulsory education regulations
that conform with those of the states where they live.

On the other hand, some more traditional Indian groups
have rebelled at efforts to close down reservation schools.
The attempt of the Bureau of Indian Affairs to close down,
on July 1, 1968, a small grade-school at Tama, Iowa, created
an instant reaction. Forty-five Mesquakie Indian children
were attending school there on the reservation purchased
by their ancestors, a separate body of the Sac tribe which,
with the Fox, had a hundred years earlier been pushed out
of Iowa into Kansas. The Mesquakie Indians, who had not
been consulted about the closing of the school, promptly
sought judicial relief. They got it in September 1968, in the
Federal District Court at Cedar Rapids, when United States
District Court Judge Edward J. McManus ordered the
school reopened in the fall. The Mesquakie were able to
call upon a number of influential white friends in their attempt to retain their Indian school. The validity of integration into a white school system that is often both distant
from and cold toward Indian values can be questioned, as
the Mesquakie questioned it.

A similar reaction occurred in Ramah, New Mexico,
where until June 1968 there was a state public school in
which Navajo children constituted a majority. The parent
Gallup-McKinley County School Board (60 percent of
whose 12,000 students are Indians yet which had in 1970

only one Indian school board member) decided to close the Ramah school and to force the children to attend a consolidated high school at Zuñi, New Mexico, twenty miles away, or Bureau of Indian Affairs boarding schools off the reservation. The 1,500 Indian residents of the area, however, decided to resist the decision. They elected their own five-member school board on February 6, 1970. None of the five members had a high school diploma but all were rich in natural good sense. With the aid of the DNA—a Navajo legal services organization—they got Bureau funds for a contract under which they would operate the first locally controlled Indian high school in the country. Whether the experiment will succeed or fail will be known later. But the action illustrates the point made by Peterson Zah, Deputy Director of DNA, that "there can be no alternative to local education of Indians." The possibility of local education of Indians under the Johnson-O'Malley Act has not been realized because the large school districts—often controlled by whites even in Indian areas—have tended to perpetuate the impersonal education familiar to the Indian student in the old Bureau schools. The involvement of Indian parents in the educational process is—in the eyes of some Indian reformers—vital. . . .

As Indian education on the elementary and secondary level achieves increasing Indian involvement, the number of Indians going on to college has increased dramatically. In 1966, 120 Indians graduated from four-year colleges and universities, double the number graduating five years before that. In 1970, 4,500 Indians were estimated to be in attendance at institutions of higher education. The Bureau of Indian Affairs provided financial support to 3,432 students in 1969 (with grants totaling more than $3 million) of which number 241 graduated from college. The Bureau also assists Indians engaged in adult educational programs in more than three hundred communities.

EDUCATION VS. ASSIMILATION [2]

I've been reading a batch of New Year's resolutions written by Navaho schoolchildren. They live in such remote fastnesses as Lukachukai Valley, Coalmine Mesa and Wide Ruins, but their resolutions are in the American mainstream.

Evelyn Mailboy writes, "I really want to learn. I really want to study. I don't want to sit around." Della Mae Begaye promises, "I'll not be lazy. . . . I'll not sleep in class. I'll listen." Larry Benally resolves to "Work hard. . . . Try to do my best in each subject." Such pledges might have been made by young Tom Edison, or by immigrant children reaching for a star in the bourgeois firmament.

True, they may merely be mouthings of children long accustomed to satisfying the peculiar demands of authority while keeping their own counsel. Yet Indians have always seemed eager to learn whatever the white man has been willing to teach. "Father," the Seneca leader Cornplanter pleaded with President Washington, "we ask that you teach us to plough and grind corn . . . and above all that you will teach our children to read and write."

Alas, we have done neither very well, mainly because we have always confused education with assimilation. It is an old story: Our schools have been a malevolent melting pot for absorbing any culture, any group, suspected of being unique.

In the case of the Indians, the process of Americanization has been especially cruel. From the beginning our policy was to kill as many Indians as conscience and firepower would allow, then whitewash the rest by means of special schools and churches. (Note that "Ten Little Indians," unlike "One Two, Buckle My Shoe" and other counting rhymes, begins at the top and works down to, "And then there were none.")

[2] From "Whitewashing the Indians," by Richard J. Margolis, author. *New Leader.* 53:13-14. D. 28, '70. Reprinted with permission from *The New Leader* of December 18, 1970. Copyright © The American Labor Conference on International Affairs, Inc.

For four centuries—ever since the Jesuits established a mission school for Florida Indians in 1568—white missionaries have preached ethnic pieties and white schools have practiced a gentleman's genocide. "The purpose of Indian schools," declared the Reverend Eleazar Wheelock, who founded Dartmouth College in 1769, "is to free Indian children from the language and habits of their untutored and oftentimes savage parents." [See "A Symbol Passes," in Section II, above.]

In order to "free" Indian children, we stole them from their tribes and families and shipped them to boarding schools far from home. Once exiled, the children were forbidden to speak their tribal languages or to practice their religion on pain of instant and brutal punishment. Recently an anthropologist in California offered to pay an elderly Indian woman, a member of the Hupa tribe, to help him transcribe the old Hupa language. For an answer the woman rolled up a sleeve and revealed a horribly twisted arm. "When I was a little child," she said, "my teacher broke this arm because I'd talked Indian. Now you say you'll pay me for doing the same thing."

Many arms and many tribes have been broken, but somehow the Indians have survived. Like the Jews of old, they will neither recant nor assimilate. Plymouth Rock is their Wailing Wall. Yet one wonders how much longer they can endure. . . .

A 1944 House [of Representatives] Select Committee on Indian Affairs offered recommendations on achieving "the final solution of the Indian problems." Boarding schools were thought to be the key. "The goal of Indian education," noted the Committee, twanging Wheelock's bowstring, "should be to make the Indian child a better American rather than to equip him simply to be a better Indian."

It never occurred to the congressmen that the two goals might be compatible; in fact, inseparable. There is no way to educate an Indian child other than through, and with respect for, his Indian-ness.

In the nineteenth century the Choctaws and the Cherokees educated their own children. Thanks to the Cherokee
scholar Sequoya's invention of an alphabet in 1821, and to
a strong tribal constitution, the Cherokees created "the finest
school system west of the Mississippi River" (according to
Senator Edward Kennedy's [Democrat, Massachusetts] Subcommittee on Indian Education). In those days 90 percent
of the Cherokee nation was literate in two languages. Together with the Choctaws it established more than two hundred schools and sent many graduates to eastern colleges.

But in 1906 the Federal Government abolished the whole
system and substituted white-controlled schools. . . . In consequence, 40 per cent of today's Cherokee adult population
is functionally illiterate; in many public schools the Cherokee dropout rate runs as high as 75 per cent.

The Cherokee disaster is an American tragedy, reflecting
as it does our lack of faith in the democratic process. The
great strength of the Cherokee school system was that it was
managed by Cherokees. Today, as anthropologist Willard
Walker has pointed out, Cherokees view the school "as a
white man's institution over which parents have no control."

We have a lot to learn about pluralism, about live-and-
let-live, and Indians can teach us. When Barboncito, the
Navaho warrior, was captured by white solders in 1868, he
said to his captors, "I hope to God you will not ask me to
go to any other country except my own. . . ." But schools
are another country for most Indian children.

Education by exile is an American custom, and Indian
children have not been the only victims. Dr. Leonard Covel-
lo, New York City's first Italo-American school principal,
recalls what it was like to attend public schools seventy
years ago:

> During this period the Italian language was completely ig-
> nored. . . . In fact, throughout my whole elementary school career,
> I do not recall the mention of Italy or of the Italian language or
> what famous Italians had done in the world. . . . We soon got the
> idea that *Italian* meant something inferior. . . . We were becoming
> Americans by learning how to be ashamed of our parents.

Has anything changed since then? Recently a teacher asked an eight-year-old Zuñi boy in New Mexico to draw a picture of his community. At the bottom of his sheet the boy drew a typical pueblo cluster; a ladder reached up toward a yellow blob, the sun, which in Zuñi tradition is the source of all power. The sun was vertically striped. And at the very top of the page, reigning over all, was a small American flag.

"But why," asked the teacher, "have you put stripes over the sun?"

"Don't you see?" came the answer. "The sun is behind bars."

PROGRESS IN HIGHER EDUCATION [3]

Conrad Black Bear and Leo Her Many Horses are studying toward degrees in business administration. Jim Kaulay is taking courses in mental-health counseling, while Collins Horselooking is working on a degree in social services. All four men are Sioux Indians and, until recently, all of them were educational dropouts. Now, they have resumed their studies at two unique community colleges—the Lakota Higher Education Center and Sinte Gleska College—on reservations in South Dakota. Black Bear, twenty-six, who left the reservation a decade ago and enrolled briefly in the University of Hawaii, says he returned "to find myself. I had lost what Indian culture I had," he explains. "But I could never learn at a big university, and I feel more comfortable here."

In the entire United States, there are only three institutions of higher education run for Indians by Indians. The third, Navajo Community College in Chinle, Arizona, was founded in 1968. Lakota (named after one of the Sioux languages) and Sinte Gleska (the Sioux name for Spotted Tail, one of the last great chiefs) are even newer, established in 1969 and 1970, respectively. Unlike the Navajo college, the South Dakota schools do not have central campuses. Instead, they have set up facilities in a dozen communities scattered

[3] From "For Indians, by Indians." *Newsweek.* 81:71-2. F. 12, '73. Copyright Newsweek, Inc. 1973, reprinted by permission.

across the five thousand square miles of rugged country that make up the adjoining Rosebud and Pine Ridge reservations. Altogether, Lakota and Sinte Gleska serve nearly one thousand full- and part-time students, offering a curriculum that ranges from academic and vocational subjects to courses in "Indian studies" drawn up under the guidance of tribal leaders, including medicine men.

The need for post-secondary education on the reservations could hardly be more pressing. The closest state colleges are 150 wind-swept miles away. Less than 1 per cent of the nineteen Sioux on the reservations have earned college degrees. Unemployment runs at roughly 40 per cent of the work force, and the average annual income is a paltry $2,000. "For two hundred years, the white man has promised to educate the Indian, and especially in terms of higher education—he has failed," charges Ray Howe, director of the Lakota Center and himself three-fourths Oglala Sioux. "Now, the people really feel they've got something they can call their own."

Funded largely by the Federal Government and grants from private foundations, the two schools offer associate-of-arts degrees in general studies and a host of career fields. They also operate agricultural departments and adult-education programs. The colleges hope to qualify Indians for the jobs and construction contracts on the reservations that now go almost entirely to non-Indians.

Most of the courses are taught by Indians, and the academic standards are high. "Some Indian students who had been getting A's at some of the smaller state colleges were quite surprised when they began getting C's here," says Gerald Mohatt, a white man who this week will hand over the directorship of Sinte Gleska to a full-blooded Sioux. "You don't get through this college because you're an Indian. You get through because you're a student."

The schools are also making a determined effort to incorporate the Sioux culture into the curriculum. The expertise comes from people like Stanley Red Bird, a rancher who serves as a professor of the Sioux language and as chairman of the Sinte Gleska board of governors. By teaching both the old and the new, Mohatt says, the college hopes to create "a new Indian culture based on the best of both worlds. Most Indian people, . . . believe reservation life and education are a one-way street pointing down. But the college is showing there is quality education here."

So determined are the two schools to remain uniquely Indian that neither has sought formal accreditation from the North Central Association. Instead, their courses are accredited through cooperating white institutions, such as the University of Colorado. "The North Central Association does not know how to evaluate a community college on a reservation," says Howe. "It requires you to have a central campus, for example, and that simply wouldn't work on the reservation." As an alternative to plugging into a white institution, the two colleges are currently exploring the possibility of forming a consortium of Indian schools for accrediting and lobbying purposes. "One of these days," declares Stanley Red Bird, "we will create a nation of Indian colleges."

REMODELING INDIAN SCHOOLS [4]

Experts have a touching faith in education, but Indians don't cotton to our white education at all. Their school dropout rates are high. "Achievement" rates are low. Indian students are, as a rule, just not interested in the kind of schools we provide for them. This bewildering problem has divided the experts into two camps.

One camp, made up generally of experts with a nationwide point of view, believes we should reconstruct Indian education to fit the Indian world.

The other camp, made up generally of experts concerned with the operation of local school districts, thinks we should keep hacking away at Indian children to carve them to fit into the pattern of our white education.

[4] From "The American Indians: The Un-Americans," by William Brandon, free-lance writer. *Progressive.* 34:35-9. Ja. '70. Reprinted by permission.

Until now the bureaucrats have won, and they fully expect to keep on winning. But it is impressive that after these many years of force-fed misfit education so many Indians are still resisting. In 1966, some 10,000 to 16,000—statistics differ —Indian children between the ages of eight and sixteen— somewhere about 10 per cent of the total US Indian school-age population of some 150,000—were out of school altogether. For some this was because no schools were available, but for many others, even though few Indian parents these days will admit it, it must be considered a deliberate withholding. The modern period in Indian statistics is neatly bracketed by the dates of 1891, when three Kiowa schoolboys froze to death trying to get home across blizzard-swept plains after running away from school, and 1967, when two Navajo students died in precisely the same way.

There is involved a clash, a conflict so profound that it takes place in the soul's least conscious depths. Our school system is naturally built to our own scale of values, "competitive, exploitative, oriented to acquisition, and above all to individual success," in the words of Dr. Anne Smith, Santa Fe anthropologist and author of several works on Indian education in New Mexico. But these values are directly opposed to the gods of the Indian world. The inherent Indian orientation is toward a sense of community, interpersonal harmony, group endeavor and achievement, rather than isolated endeavor and individual achievement. To the Indian child therefore our schools are likely to seem either silly or hostile, as he comes to realize they are teaching false values compared to the values learned at home.

A number of recent studies have disclosed that the Indian family usually presents to the schools, a stable, well-adjusted, willing, quick-learning child, who does splendidly at first, and then, at about the fourth or fifth grade, begins to regress. By the time he finishes high school—60 per cent drop out along the way—he has acquired less than a tenth-grade education. Many teachers have commented on the typical Indian child in kindergarten, so outgoing and happy and friendly,

who turns into the withdrawn, rather apprehensive child
of later grades. Clearly, he approaches the big outside world
ready for a joyous embrace, and the big outside world grad-
ually infects his spirit with the nightmare sickness of finding
one's self out of kilter with a world one expected to love.

Worst of all, since the children danced into this invisible
chasm of alienness without any idea that it is there, each
child thinks his "failure" must mean there is something
wrong with him personally. A 1966 Government report much
quoted by educators (the Coleman Report) revealed that
twelfth-grade Indian students chose for themselves bottom
rank in answers to the question, "How bright do you think
you are?"

Not surprisingly, this misfit educational system long ago
lost interest in its apathetic child victims; its "goals" are for
the benefit of the system, not the students. Prison-like boarding schools were established for easier administrative effi-
ciency, better living conditions for the staff, convenience in
using the visual-aid gadgets that to the superficial mind define "quality education." These children's concentration
camps have come in for flaming criticism, much of it from
white patriots alleging the Indian schools were slowing down
"assimilation" by keeping Indian children fenced off from
the melting pot. So, in 1965-66, the Government asked Indians what they thought of taking Indian children away
from the Bureau of Indian Affairs and its segregated schools.
Some younger Indians favored this, but most tribal spokesmen protested vehemently, less from love for the BIA schools
than from opposition to the rejected goal of assimilation.

The Government thereupon carried out the vetoed proposal anyway but without saying so, and while education
is still big business . . . in the BIA, two thirds of all Indian
pupils have been quietly transferred to public schools, where
Federal funds pay for them by the head. . . .

"We teach exactly the same courses and use exactly the
same textbooks as all other Arizona schools," said the superintendent of the handsome new elementary and high school

on the Papago reservation in the desert country of southern Arizona. He was caustic about "Indian values" that were supposedly worth "saving." "My parents came from Denmark," he said. "They did not teach us children Danish. They were happy to come to this fine country with all its great and wonderful opportunities. They wanted us children to appreciate America and be Americans." The superintendent all but implied that if the Indians didn't like this fine country they should go back where they came from.

Related to the central misfit problem are various other handicaps—language, for one. Classes are usually conducted in English although two thirds of the children know no English at all when they begin school.

Our "best" people think nothing can be finer for their own children than a bilingual education in French, but an Indian child is generally regarded as "disadvantaged" by red and white alike because he speaks Cherokee or Ojibwa or Tsimshian—this, even though it is beginning to be recognized that Indian languages possess their own literatures, often literatures of beauty and sophistication. But the effects of the "primitive language" misconception will long remain, especially among the ignorant who speak of all Indian languages as "Indian dialects.". . .

Even though our Indian education is, plainly, misfitted to basic Indian culture, it can still train students in technical and professional skills. Despairing Indian parents see no way out of a poverty future for their children except to force them into the schools, and some Indian students do survive to remain tribal people while becoming university-trained doctors, lawyers, or Indian chiefs. Yet some are left hopelessly deformed; some are trapped by the alien gods and find themselves "assimilated." Most, however, reject the education that is so foreign to their real world: The average Indian ends his formal education with just five years of school.

A faint hope has sprung up among deeply concerned Indian experts that the practice of carving an Indian child to fit the white educational system may be overthrown. Their hope is based mainly on the work of the special United States Senate Subcommittee on Indian Education, the "Kennedy Committee" first chaired by [the late] Senator Robert Kennedy [Democrat, New York] later by Senator Edward Kennedy [Democrat, Massachusetts]. The subcommittee's final report, presented early in November 1969, offers sixty concrete recommendations designed to bring about "culturally sensitive" programs and bilingual programs and increased Indian control of Indian education. It calls for a White House conference and a Senate Select Committee to see that these basic changes are really made. Throughout the 2,371 pages of testimony, the opinion prevails that the present destructive schooling should cease and that education for Indians should be totally redirected to fit the outlook of the Indian world, to "strengthen and develop and ennoble" the Indian social structure rather than oppose it, as the subcommittee testimony quotes expert Bruce Gaarder of the United States Office of Education.

The obvious first move toward achieving the goal is simply to let Indians run their own schools, or, in the case of mixed schools, to serve on school boards more proportionally than is now the case.

Another obvious move is toward bilingual education. This can serve both the welfare of Indian students and the welfare of Indian languages, inextricably bound up together. . . .

A reconstruction of Indian education around the fundamental structures of the Indian world—a world of living together, rather than striving against one another for acquisitions, a world of community—might conceivably offer a vestibule to reconstruction of Indian education even in our mainstream world.

V. THE INDIAN IN HIS OWN SETTING

EDITOR'S INTRODUCTION

When the typical non-Indian American thinks about Indians, the first picture that inevitably comes to mind is the colorful portrait of the native American in his own setting— Indians by and for themselves, within a reservation, steeped in their own customs, culture, and philosophy. And that is, indeed, vitally important in studying the American Indian of the 1970s. This section attempts to depict this aspect of Indian life, with the tribalism of ancient days sweeping in one continuous flow to the tribal life and enterprise of today —and very likely of tomorrow.

The rediscovery of the Indian in his own culture is described from a historical viewpoint by Professor Howard R. Lamar. An examination of the Indian community by William Brandon follows.

Industry Week tells the story of the coordination of the reservation and industry, hopefully to their joint benefit. The section concludes with modern-day portraits of four Indian tribes, each distinctly different from the others—first, Alvin Josephy's moving homage to the Hopis; and, then, up-to-date reports on the Navajos, Zuñis, and Jicarilla Apaches.

A TIME OF REDISCOVERY [1]

The Old West, romantic and heroic, has in two decades become the area which epitomizes the most basic questions facing American society today.

[1] From "The New Old West," by Howard R. Lamar, professor of American history, Yale University. *Yale Alumni Magazine*. 36:7-15. O. '72. Reprinted with permission from the October 1972 issue of the *Yale Alumni Magazine*; copyright by Yale Alumni Publications, Inc.

The emergence of a "new" historical West struck me . . . as I listened to a Yale junior give a fine report on Handsome Lake, a Seneca Indian whose religious teachings had rejuvenated the spirit and culture of his tribe at the close of the eighteenth century. In the discussion which followed, the class drew comparisons with religious revivals led by Tenskwatawa, the Shawnee prophet, and by Wovoka, leader of the Ghost Dance religion. Then the talk jumped ahead to the comparatively recent rise of the peyote cult and of the Native American Church. The students noted that in our time Indian religious movements were taking place which bore a clear resemblance to the older ones.

The interest in Handsome Lake was symbolic of the changes of emphasis which have occurred in the course. Ten years ago the student probably would have reported on New Deal Indian policy; twenty years ago he would have talked about an Indian war or Custer's "Last Stand." In less than ten years Indians have become in white eyes—and in history courses—peoples, societies and cultures. Today the Yale student's effort to understand the historical Indian goes far beyond a romantic concept of the noble savage, or a guilt feeling engendered by Dee Brown's *Bury My Heart at Wounded Knee* and Thomas Berger's *Little Big Man*, although these books may have stimulated his interest. This mature attitude of seeking to understand people and societies has turned most traditionally narrative history courses into ones on social process. . . .

The most impressive change . . . has been the rediscovery of the American Indian. The ranges of that rediscovery seem boundless. New archeological evidence, pouring in from all over North America, suggests that the whole history of pre-Columbian Indian population movements and societies must be rewritten. All the population figures which once implied that the whites came to an empty continent are under challenge. Did white diseases destroy Indian society before the average settler came? And what of life and customs in those societies? A few years ago Edmund Morgan described the Atlantic Coast Indians of the Colonial period as incorrigible individualists who were extremely indulgent and permissive in their child-rearing practices. . . . The old assumption that the Indians had no sense of history or of the past is also about to go out the window.

Other scholars have discovered that the so-called stupidity and backwardness of California tribes was actually a kind of Quaker pacificism which citizen and expert alike have misinterpreted. Roy Harvey Pearce, in his fine study of the image of the Indian in the American mind, has found that we have used the Indian to define what we, as a Protestant middle-class society, feared, hated or considered taboo. Today that image has been so reversed that the Indian is in danger of becoming a twentieth century noble savage who has a monopoly on understanding nature, is a born conservationist and is possessed of a superior spirit.

The emergence of a new and more rewarding approach to Indians is not just a fad or a show of tolerance implying a triumph over racism. Recent studies also suggest that Americans, from the founding of Plymouth Plantation, have been fascinated by the Indian way of life. We now learn that many people who were captured by Indians willingly stayed on as part of an Indian family. In that discovery we learn things about ourselves as well as about the Indian. And as we take a more open look at past students of Indians we find that there was an honorable tradition of men and women, from John Eliot to Oliver LaFarge and John Collier, who understood and admired them. . . .

The clear fact is that the whole of Indian history and of Indian-white relations must be rewritten in terms of what we have recently learned about premodern societies and race relations. This rewriting comes at a crucial moment when the "New Indians"—Indian intellectual and political leaders (that phrase by itself represents a revolution in our thinking)—are defining their own values and have launched a Pan-Indian movement. [See "Pan-Indianism," in Section VII, below.] Without even trying, then, the tra-

ditional Western history course has in the last . . . [few]
years become a course on culture and race relations as we
witness a highly articulate twentieth century generation of
secular Handsome Lakes attempting to restore the spirit of
a people.

THE INDIAN COMMUNITY [2]

A young Indian girl . . . [at the University of California,
Berkeley] told me that in saying goodby to her old-fashioned
parents—her mother in blanket and high moccasins, her
father in sober, tall, black sombrero—she had felt she was
leaving them as far behind as on another planet, because
she was becoming a "catalyst of rebellion" in the Third
World Liberation Front. Yet the objectives she would fight
for with the TWLF—more money, better jobs, even the
grand objective of seizing power, were the usual and proper
aims of the apple-pie American world. Her tribal parents,
inhabiting a world of truly different dimensions, uninterest-
ed in proper American values, not even interested in seizing
power, were, it seemed to me, the real revolutionaries of her
family, absorbed in an authentic revolutionary movement:
their Indian community.

The radical character of the Indian world is most easily
discernible in its sense of community, a community identity
originally founded on the custom of communal ownership:
ownership of land in common by a related group of people
is one of the few traits that might be applied sweepingly to
nearly all American Indians throughout the hemisphere.
This community superlife based on a communal ownership
still frequently in evidence, is the unique quality of the
Indian world. It is an attitude truly revolutionary for our
present world, which rather derives from the Old World
kingship pattern—public domain regarded as the property
of a ruling government apparatus, a notion prevailing in
most modern states, socialist or Communist included.

[2] From "American Indians: The Real American Revolution," by William
Brandon, author of *The American Heritage Book of Indians. Progressive.* 34:
26-30. F. '70. Reprinted by permission.

In the true communal ownership of Indian tradition, each member of the community has an "absolute and complete" right of actual ownership, as the United States Court of Claims held in an 1893 opinion later sustained by the United States Supreme Court. "Chiefs and headmen" have no authority to dispose of these rights, and even a majority of the tribe or community has no authority to sell the communal property, which would seem to constitute, said the Court, "taking away the property of the minority and disposing of it without their consent."

The communal point of view has always been difficult for the private-ownership mentality to grasp. The 1893 Court remarked that this difficulty was no doubt at the bottom of "many of our troubles with the Indian tribes." It still is. It is the alien ness of this communal identity that elicits much of our harassment (conscious and unconscious) of the Indian world, that puts Indian children at odds with our schools, and that fires the pressures for "termination" of Federal protection of Indian groups with the ultimate objective of forcing the collapse of the Indian communities, compelling their people to disperse and, at last, to become "assimilated" in our own competitive culture.

Although Indian leaders, too, give lip service to the pious aims of more money and better jobs, these are acceptable only on the Indian community's terms. The people of an Indian community generally will not sell out for individual opportunities no matter how alluring, will undergo any privations to remain part of their living community. The community superlife, calling for interpersonal harmony rather than interpersonal striving, is in absolute opposition to the orthodox American gods of work-as-a-virtue and amassing personal wealth as the measure of success. . . .

Will we, can we, permit this revolutionary world to go on ticking away in our midst? The obvious response is that of course we can and of course we should—we should, in fact, do everything in our power to aid its survival. The continuing Indian revolution is essential to the health of our own world in more ways than one: not only in providing our democracy with the oxygen of a truly alien presence, but in keeping alive that heartbeat of community so strong in the Indian world, so feeble in our own, so necessary, possibly, to the survival of us all. . . .

The whole spectrum of differences between an Indian community in action and a non-Indian community in action would repay the most serious large-scale study. Newly evolving forms of tribal government, usually including closed-membership corporations or reasonable facsimiles thereof, may bear resemblances now and then to white corporations —the same investment counselors and tax counselors may be hired by both—but in essence they are novel structures because they are built on foundations that are different, alien, foundations shaped by the tradition of communal ownership.

Most concrete Indian successes are realized in group terms—tribal cattle herds, or the communal big business of recreation on some reservations, such as the $1.5 million complex being built by the Crows in Montana, at Yellowtail Dam on the Bighorn. Or spectacularly in land: The financial renaissance within no more than ten years of the Cheyenne River Sioux in South Dakota (they now operate, among other things, a cattle business, sales pavilion, supermarket, and their own telephone company serving Indians and non-Indians in two counties) grew mainly from initial successes with a tribal land-consolidation program. The Tribal Land Enterprise agency of the Rosebud Sioux in South Dakota buys land at a rate reaching a quarter-million dollars a year, and the land-consolidation program of the Crows has reached a half-million dollars' worth a year.

But these occasional successes have barely made a dent in the massive Indian poverty. . . . The much-publicized project of bringing industry to the reservations has made another dent, somewhat offset by the fact that the main pitch to industry has been low capital cost and cheap labor, scarcely conducive to blue-chip deals; and even seamier considerations have appeared here and there, as in current efforts to thrust a giant paper mill upon Isleta Pueblo, New Mexico, so as to sidestep anti-pollution rules set up by the state (Indian land isn't subject to state control).

It will take more than dents to remedy reservation poverty—it will take a solid breakthrough in giving back to the Indian communities sufficient land to live on. At present, the process is still going the wrong direction: Indian lands and resources are still being whittled away. Land-consolidation operations financed by the Indians themselves cannot possibly fill the required bill. The nation simply needs to honor its given word in securing to the Indian communities a livable land base. Nothing less will work.

INDUSTRY ON THE RESERVATION [3]

American Indians are on the warpath again—but this time they're after industrial and economic development. Their goal: convincing industry it makes economic sense to locate plants and other facilities on Indian reservations. And their story has many companies taking a second look at the possibility.

"It amazes me when I see American companies setting up factories all over the world because they think they can't afford to manufacture here in the United States," explains Robert L. Friedlander, vice president of Chicago's Thomas H. Miner & Associates Inc.

As Mr. Friedlander sees it, "there's no need for industry to go to Taiwan when it can find many of the same advantages on an Indian reservation."

One of the biggest advantages, of course, is the huge pool of available labor. On many reservations unemployment currently stands at 70 or 80 percent, so there's no problem finding sufficient numbers of workers.

Wage rates are also a definite plus factor. Many firms' average salaries are well below $2 per hour, explains Mr. Friedlander.

[3] From "Firms Find Indian Reservation Is Good Place to Locate Plant." *Industry Week*. 171:14-16. O. 18, '71. Reprinted by permission.

However, many firms also wonder whether unskilled Indians can work in industry. For example, Ute Fabricating Company, Fort Duchesne, Utah, found that many of its Indian job applicants "had less than one year's total work experience in their lives," explains Richard N. Jones, the firm's general manager.

Fairchild Camera & Instrument Corporation's Semiconductor Division, which built a plant on a reservation in Shiprock, New Mexico, faced a similar situation; almost all of its Indian applicants had no industrial experience at all.

For both firms, the skills problem turned out to be no problem at all.

For one thing, there are millions of dollars in Federal training funds available to companies, says an official of the United States Department of Commerce's Economic Development Administration (EDA).

"The Bureau of Indian Affairs, the Department of Labor, the Office of Economic Opportunity, and other agencies all have training programs," explains Edward Huiszingh, EDA program specialist for Indian affairs. In addition, some of the Indian tribes themselves have special programs.

And, as Fairchild Camera's management found, "Although the Indians had no experience, that also meant they had no bad work habits. They were very receptive and developed excellent work habits," points out George Higgins, the plant's manager of employee relations.

At Fairchild, in fact, Indian workers proved they can easily fit into the industrial environment. "Our Shiprock plant has the most complex product mix in the company," explains Mr. Higgins, who adds that the firm has also established a precise machining shop there—staffed by trained Indians. The plant's productivity is as high as or higher than any other plant in the firm.

Another advantage to manufacturing on an Indian reservation is the many other assistance programs available from the tribes and various Government agencies. These programs can help firms in everything from plant construction to worker housing.

Don't forget joint ventures. As Harold Culbertson, executive director of Standing Rock Industries, Standing Rock, on the North and South Dakota border, explains, "there are literally millions of dollars available for joint ventures with Indian groups."

And finally, there's a sales advantage. As minority businesses, these joint ventures get preferential treatment on some Government contracts.

Obviously, there are problems in manufacturing on reservations, but most firms have found they can be overcome. The transportation situation differs from reservation to reservation. Although thirty reservations currently have developed industrial parks with good roads and rail facilities, others in fact are miles from anywhere.

Ute Fabricating faced the latter situation; so did Fairchild, but to a lesser degree. However, both firms found that careful planning of inventories and efficient ordering techniques negated almost all transportation problems.

Another problem centers on the Indians' social structures, which may require firms to modify certain personnel policies. For example, Indians have their own religious customs and special holidays, which have to be considered. Also there's the Indians' relaxed conception of time. Some firms have worried that Indians wouldn't be able to meet delivery dates and schedules, but Ute Fabricating's Mr. Jones has found that "all it takes is explanation. We've never been late on a shipment."

"When you consider the advantages and disadvantages, you've got to admit that manufacturing on a reservation is an untapped idea for industry," claims Miner & Associates' Mr. Friedlander.

"The electronics industry seems aware of the potential, but most other industries haven't even thought about reservations," he adds.

James E. Mohrhauser, president, Versa Technologies, Inc., Racine, Wisconsin, agrees, adding that "I'm afraid most firms are totally ignorant of the enormous opportunities Indian reservations can offer. As far as I can see, transportation looks like the biggest problem today, but that doesn't scare me a bit. Trucking firms are darn aggressive. If there's a need, they'll respond."

Indian leaders are taking their story to industry, and they're sure industry will listen—especially in today's economic climate.

THE HOPI WAY [4]

Perched on the edge of a rocky mesa six hundred feet above the desert of northeastern Arizona is the Hopi Indian village of Hotevilla. A stronghold of Hopi traditionalists—Indians who remain profoundly loyal to the religious teachings and values of their ancestors—the little settlement of fewer than a thousand people is something of an anachronism on the American scene, a remnant of another day and another way of life that defies many of the influences of the white man's modern-day civilization and at the same time challenges it to do as well in providing mankind with enduring answers for an existence of happiness and contentment.

To the visitor Hotevilla appears to have some of the attributes of a true-life Shangri-la. One of twelve Hopi villages that are strung, at an altitude of six thousand feet, for some seventy miles along the southern escarpment of Black Mesa, it is a remarkable center of peace and serenity in a vast, silent land of stone cliffs and canyons, sandy wastes, and huge, dramatic stretches of painted desert. From a distance the town, like all the Hopi villages, seems to be a part of the landscape, the shapes and earth colors of the buildings blending with the rough terrain of the mesa top. The settlement is low and compact. Rows of flattopped stone buildings,

[4] From an article by Alvin M. Josephy, Jr., author and senior editor, Book Division, American Heritage Publishing Company. *American Heritage.* 24:49-55. F. '73. © 1973 by American Heritage Publishing Company, Inc. Reprinted by permission from *American Heritage,* February, 1973.

some with two or three tiers, front on narrow sandy streets. In large open plazas are mounds of earth, covering kivas, the Hopis' underground religious and social rooms, which are reached by ladders whose tops protrude from holes in the center of the mounds. Foxskins and bundles of feathers, part of the garb for the annual round of ceremonial dances and rituals, hang from the walls of some of the buildings.

The town is busy but quiet. Men with bangs over their foreheads and with their long hair in back tied up with a string work industriously repairing houses or packing wool sheared from their flocks of sheep into bags for market. Children and dogs romp past them. Women with pails of water or arms full of corn shuffle by. They have come up steep paths that lead from springs and gardens far below the mesa's edge. From the lip of the mesa the view of the green patches of terraced gardens and the broad desert floor stretching into the distance is at once breathtaking and idyllic. Each garden plot, bordered by a stone wall around it, has been given to a family by the *kikmongwi*, the hereditary chief and spiritual leader of the village. The sandy lower slopes and valleys beneath the mesa are dotted with the dark green clusters of growing crops: squash, beans, melons, gourds, and cotton, as well as corn. Among and beyond the plots, extending in isolated little clumps of green across the desert, are peach trees. Summer rains and seepage from springs water the garden plots, winter rains and snow help the fruit trees. Above the gardens, on a bench of land part way down the mesa wall, a spring feeds a large pool from which the village women fill their pails.

All is outwardly quiet, harmonious, and contented. It is the routine of ages, but there is no sign of monotony. Nothing shrill breaks the peace—no quarreling, no anger. In the silence of the humans and the spaciousness of the unspoiled land one is aware of a closeness to nature: the presence of earth and rocks and growing things everywhere; the clambering down to the gardens and the clambering back up; the vastness of the view from the mesa; the dramatic

thunderstorms, the dust clouds, and the movement of the
sun that brings changing colors to the canyon walls; the
rain, the springs, and the pool of water on which everything
depends. But there is also a meticulous order here, day upon
day, year after year, that comes from an unquestioned de-
votion to a timeless philosophy and plan of life. The well-
spring of the plan was nature. Its author, the traditionalist
Hopis say, was a god, and its goal is to help man to be good
so that he will not destroy himself. . . .

A new interest in America's minority groups has made
the Indians the subject of many books, magazine articles,
movies, and television programs, and accounts of their cultures are having an impact on a restless and changing world.
To the disturbed and dissatisfied who are searching for new
values and life-styles and for better relationships with their
fellow men, the supernatural, and the earth, almost all the
original Indian cultures arouse images of a more natural
—and therefore a purer and more self-fulfilling—existence.
But most of the native cultures have long since vanished, or
been changed by the white man. Here and there in the
Western Hemisphere tribes exist with much of the content
of their original cultures intact, or almost so, but none of
them are as accessible to outsiders as the Hopis, whose centuries-old beliefs are still carefully guarded and maintained
by the traditionalists.

Today visitors to the mesa villages are coming in large
numbers—husbands and wives and whole families, longhairs
in vans, single girls and groups of women, professional men
fed up with urban life, and television crews from the United
States and abroad—trailing to the stone houses of the gray-
haired Hopi elders for interviews and discussions and attending the clans' religious observances in the plazas, studying in awed silence the rituals. . . .

Not all the Hopis are traditionalists and participate in
the clan ceremonies. . . . Government schools and Christian
churches established in some of the villages have turned
many of the people away from the beliefs and ways of their

ancestors. Known as progressives, to contrast them with the conservatives, or traditionalists, they live like white men and raise and educate their children to be successful in the white man's world. But many of them are defensive and know that they retain Hopi values that they will never shed, and some of their children, becoming militantly antiwhite, have gone over to the traditionalists and eagerly sought instruction in the old ways.

The traditionalists exist in every village, though they are strongest at Hotevilla, which they founded in 1906 after a split in another village, Oraibi, between themselves and those who wished to follow the ways of the white man. To the outsider there is ample evidence that the traditionalists themselves have not found all of those new ways bad. They have welcomed the material comforts and conveniences of modern civilization and, as individuals, have made choices of what to accept and what to reject. Sewing machines, canned foods, automobiles, and Grand Rapids furniture are among many of the white man's products that are commonplace on the mesas. But the people of Hotevilla have kept electricity out of the village and have no sewerage. To some it makes no sense; to the traditionalists who made the choices such decisions had a relationship to what really mattered— not the adoption of material conveniences, but the maintenance of age-old beliefs and values and the opposition to changes that might tend to undermine and destroy those values. They will drive everywhere in automobiles, wear sunglasses to protect their eyes, and use dime-store supplies for a hundred practical needs. Why no electricity in Hotevilla? It may baffle an outsider. But the traditionalist has considered, and has rebuffed what he believes to be a threat. There is only one thing important to him: in his home and clan kiva the Hopi must keep alive the myths, legends, and prophecies on which rests the pattern of his life. It is an intertwining of religion and philosophy that he calls "the Hopi Way."

NAVAJOS—A CHANGING TRIBE [5]

Definition of a Navajo family: papa, mama, four children—and an anthropologist. The Navajo nation is one of the most studied of Indian tribes. It has been under a thousand sociological microscopes.

Of all the Indian reservations it is the biggest—25,000 square miles—as big geographically as West Virginia, and scattered across parts of three western states (Arizona, Utah, and New Mexico).

Of all the Indian populations it is the largest—130,000. No other tribe can come close. One of every five Indians in America is a Navajo.

Of all the Indian enclaves, it is the closest to being a sovereign nation or state. Of all the Indian tribes it is nearest to being an "establishment."

The Navajos are a changing people. While holding to a traditional past full of sheepherding, rug weaving, and craftmaking, they are stepping gingerly off in directions new to them. And in the seventies, "the decade of the Indian," the Navajos by dint of sheer size and geography will be the tribe most likely to evolve a new form of true minority self-determination and independence—perhaps even a special statehood.

Persistence Prevails

The Navajo first appeared on the trail toward change ... when a spell-binding Navajo politician named Raymond Nakai was elected tribal chairman. Mr. Nakai was an ordinance-depot foreman in Flagstaff, Arizona, by day and a radio announcer by night.

His rich Navajo voice became well enough known to his people that in 1954 he ran for tribal chairman. He lost, but returned in 1958 to try again—and lost again. But in

[5] From "The Navajos, Bellwether Tribe," by Jack Waugh, staff correspondent. *Christian Science Monitor.* 63:9. Ja. 8, '71. Reprinted by permission from *The Christian Science Monitor.* © 1971 The Christian Science Publishing Society. All rights reserved.

1962 he won. And admiring whites who know him insist he has modernized the reservation.

The dogged Mr. Nakai made industrialization of the reservations the chief cornerstone of his administration. The "Little Mexican" (that is *Nakai* translated) reached out into the *belagana* (white) world and courted industry. He persuaded Fairchild Camera to move its semiconductor division into Shiprock, on the reservation's northern New Mexico end. General Dynamics set up a plant in Fort Defiance on the Arizona side.

Ampex Corporation moved into Mexican Springs in New Mexico with a tennis-shoe factory. Westward Coach, a maker of mobile homes, opened a plant at Mexican Hat on the Utah side. And the tribe opened a sawmill and started its own "TVA"—the Navajo Tribal Utility Authority.

In the evening of the Nakai incumbency the Navajo Tribal Council signed agreements with Peabody Coal Company, the Salt River Project, and the Public Service Company of Arizona to mine coal at Black Mesa for a cluster of power plants in the Colorado River Basin, which enraged environmentalists and dumped Mr. Nakai into a pit of controversy.

All of these industrial moves together have made nearly five thousand jobs for Indians on the reservation. It was the golden stickpin of the Nakai years. However, it was no golden panacea.

Despite the industrialization, 65 percent of the Navajo work force is still unemployed. There are twelve thousand jobs on the reservation. And even if each job supports five Navajos, that still takes care of only half the people. There have never been enough jobs to accommodate more than half the Navajos entering the labor market each year. Some 2,500 Navajos enter the work force annually. And never have more than 1,000 new jobs been created. If that tide keeps moving unstemmed, the Navajos will be worse off in 1980 than they were in 1970.

Promise Tarnished

Besides, Mr. Nakai may have milked the industrial cow dry. At one time more than twenty industries said they were ready to come. But the Navajos could not muster the facilities. Moreover, they can't compete with big cities. A transportation system through the reservation is nonexistent. The kinds of industry adaptable to the remoteness of the life are limited.

Electronics assembly plants have been the staple. Most other industries just can't survive economically against urban competition. And that is the sorry story on virtually every reservation.

Industrialization was new to the Navajos. For centuries they had lived a simple life next to the earth. Unlike many of the Plains Indians who roamed from bluff to bluff and set up in easy-to-move tepees, and unlike the Pueblo Indians who clustered in high-walled adobe settlements, the Navajos ran to scattered individual hogans on the open windy land. They were less a nation than a leaderless band.

That was how Kit Carson, the Indian fighter, found them in 1864 when he marched into Fort Defiance at the head of the United States Cavalry. He flushed out every Navajo in every hogan he could find—about 8,400 in all—and forced them into what became known as The Long Walk to Fort Sumner, three hundred miles away in eastern New Mexico.

For three years the Navajos sat in exile, decimated by plagues and raiding Comanches, until the treaty of 1868, which established their reservation. That year what was left of the Navajos—some 6,000—made another long walk home to Fort Defiance, scattered again into hogans across the reservation and settled into a colonial life under the Bureau of Indian Affairs (BIA).

In 1921 the *belaganas* struck oil on the reservation and needed a tribal entity empowered to sign valid oil leases. Up to this time the Navajos had never had a tribal government of any kind. In fact, structured government was alien to their traditions.

Family Units Served

Until 1921 family units similar to Bennie Arviso's today were the only form of Navajo government. Mr. Arviso lives on a plot of land in a hogan at Mariano Lake, with no electricity or gas, where he has raised a family of four daughters and three sons, most of whom have married and all of whom still live in nearby hogans on the same land. For centuries Navajo family patriarchs like Bennie were the sole seats of Navajo government.

The white man, elbow deep in new-found oil, needed a central government to deal with. So one was cut out of whole cloth, structured like a parliament, with a tribal chairman and council.

The first chairman was Ohe Dodge, a famous Navajo leader. The Navajos have been electing a chairman every four years since. But tribal government did not begin to flower into bigness until the 1950s, when the oil royalties started multiplying into the millions and Navajos found themselves with a substantial treasury.

Now, running tribal government is big business. The tribal chairman has an $18,000-a-year salary and each of the seventy-eight councilmen makes $9,000—higher pay than most state legislators in the United States.

The 1971 Navajo budget tops $14 million. The tribe has even adopted the budgetary vices of white budgetmakers —deficit spending. In the past few years spending has exceeded income and is expected to again this year—by more than $1 million. Last year's initial budget of $15 million ballooned to $20 million before the fiscal year was done.

However, a quirk of Navajo budgetmaking not common to most government is declining size. Past annual tribal budgets have gone as high as $35 million.

The tribal chairman exercises massive patronage and wields it in the best Chicago ward-heeling tradition. . . .

The tribal government has only the sovereignty and power the BIA will let it exercise. And individual Navajos, in turn, have only the individual freedom that the two governments will let them have—the BIA plus the tribal structure.

Since all land on the reservation belongs to the tribe, a Navajo cannot build a hogan without a homesite permit from the tribal government. And the tribal government can't grant it if the BIA does not approve. The individual Navajo can't take up farming or graze his cattle without a Government permit. The pattern, even on the biggest and richest reservation of all, is still dominant government and submissive people.

ZUÑIS AND JICARILLA APACHES—GOING THEIR OWN WAY [6]

Two Indian tribes—the Zuñis and the Jicarilla Apaches —could hardly be more different, yet alike. Both dwell in out-of-the-way reaches of New Mexico in the shadows of towering mesas.

But the Zuñis are among the poorest Indians in the country. There are 6,000 of them and their tribal income is a meager $40,000 a year. They suffered a uranium bust.

The Jicarilla Apaches are among the richest Indians in the country. There are 1,400 of them and their annual tribal budget exceeds $2 million. They hit it rich on oil.

The Zuñis are a Pueblo tribe that has squatted on the same land for centuries, long before the first Spaniard rode up from the south, long enough to have created two hundred ancient ruins.

The Jicarillas are wanderers and fighters. About the only permanent ruins they have left are early model Chevrolet pickup trucks.

[6] From "Decolonization of the Indian," by Jack Waugh, staff correspondent. *Christian Science Monitor*. 63:9. Ja. 9, '71. Reprinted by permission from *The Christian Science Monitor*. © 1971 The Christian Science Publishing Society. All rights reserved.

The Zuñis stand among the finest silversmiths in the world. The only crafts the Jicarillas have mastered are coupon counting and high finance.

Both in their own fashions have it made. Both are prototypes of Indian success. The Zuñis made it with planning, the Jicarillas with planning—and money.

Robert E. Lewis is the short, beginning-to-paunch ex-plumber, now governor of the Zuñi Pueblo who has a great gap-toothed smile and hair that is permanently matted under his Stetson sweatband. He was first elected head of the Zuñi nation in 1964. And the first thing he tried to find out was what the Zuñis would have him do.

Christmas List Formed

He polled his people, . . . asking them to list every project they ever had wanted done. They came back with 150 different suggestions, which Mr. Lewis called the Christmas list. The tribal government picked out 24 of them and set a goal to finish them within 24 months.

The Zuñi Pueblo sits in a windy plain at the foot of sacred Corn Mountain. The clouds roll across the mountain on a typical late-autumn day and the wind whips up dust and the acrid stench of the sewer lagoons through the town. The squat Zuñi houses are hewn from the rocks of the surrounding buttes.

Nearly every house is crammed with one or more families and is topped with a TV aerial. But besides TV there is little other recreation. The nearest movie house is forty miles away in Gallup. There is no hospital in the village; it is four miles away on Black Rock, where the white contingent on the reservation lives.

The Pueblo is peppered with outdoor adobe ovens and the Zuñi women, laughing and gap-toothed like their governor, hang the wash out to dry on clotheslines. Sidewalks are nonexistent; the shawled women and the boot-clad men have learned through centuries to live with dust.

First on the governor's Christmas list was moving the sewer lagoons from upwind only a mile out of the Pueblo to a spot two miles downwind.

Among the twenty-four projects was one to lift the per capita Zuñi income from $580 a year—the lowest of any group in New Mexico—to $700. The total personal income for the 6,000 residents in the Zuñi Pueblo was $3.4 million. And a third of that was made by 903 high-salaried Bureau of Indian Affairs (BIA) employees.

Unemployment Problem

The Zuñis, beset by 30 percent unemployment, also wanted more jobs. So one of the projects was to recruit some industry. The tribal government built an industrial park on the hill at Black Rock and wooed and won an electronics-assembly plant, which has put 120 Zuñis to work.

Another plan was to levy taxes to fill the perennially empty tribal treasury.

Near the end of the twenty-four months, with the twenty-four projects nearly done, BIA officials in Washington called Governor Lewis and asked if he could meet them in Albuquerque. That was in July 1968.

President Johnson had ordered the Secretary of the Interior to pick a tribe for a pilot project in political and economic self-determination.

Washington had heard of the Zuñi twenty-four-project plan and BIA officials felt the Pueblo was isolated enough and its leadership strong enough to make a good pilot tribe.

The Zuñis would draw up a comprehensive plan. The Federal Government would underwrite the costs. But the tribe would totally run it. The BIA would withdraw and the tribe would be in full charge. It would be a total departure from the past.

A year later Governor Lewis and a quartet of BIA officials and tribal officers flew to Washington with a finished five-year plan.

It will cost $55.3 million and draw on funding from fourteen separate federal agencies. At the end of the five years forty-three projects are to be finished. Per capita income is to be lifted to $1,200. Forty commercial establishments and one shipping center are to be built at Zuñi together with 565 low-income and 150 medium-income homes.

Forty-five miles of dirt streets are to be paved. Sidewalks, gutters, and storm drains are to go in. Gas and garbage service are to be brought into 1,300 homes. Hospital capacity on the hill is to be drastically increased. A senior citizens' home is to be built. Cultural facilities are to be increased 25 percent. The teacher-pupil ratio in the Zuñi schools is to be reduced from 38 to 1 to 20 to 1. A new elementary school is to be built and a new high school. Two thousand six hundred Zuñis are to receive vocational training.

Plan Launched

Officials in Washington called the plan the finest they had ever seen. Since then it has been launched.

The Zuñis cut their ties with the BIA in a public signing ceremony . . . [in May 1970] and have been running their own affairs since. Governor Lewis, even though he still sits in an office with a big full-color photo of President Nixon and smaller black-and-white shots of the Secretary of the Interior and the Commissioner of Indian Affairs, clearly runs things.

The Zuñi government employs 120, including a brace of whites who take orders from the governor. "Nothing," says one of them, Jack Taylor, the tribe's economic development director, "is done here the Zuñis don't want done."

The program is so unique, so many necks are on the block —from the BIA's to the governor's—so many tribes are watching and failure would set back Indian affairs so far, that everybody involved is willing to work. And because of it, Mr. Taylor says, "what Zuñi wants, Zuñi gets."

The plan is critical because if it does work for the Zuñis then modifications of it are certain for scores of other Indian tribes and with it ultimate Indian economic and political self-determination. It may be the first step toward the end of colonization of the American Indian.

The Jicarillas and Oil

Charlie Vigil is cut from slightly different Indian cloth than Robert Lewis. . . .

But like Governor Lewis, Charlie Vigil leads an Indian nation—not a big one, but a rich one.

The Jicarilla Apaches didn't begin rich. They were pony-riding, war-whooping troublemakers in the middle 1800s when Kit Carson took them into captivity and packed them off to Fort Sumner in eastern New Mexico with the Navajos.

Then in the 1880s the Jicarillas were awarded 750,000 acres of reservation land in the snowpacked extremities of northern New Mexico, which looked good for nothing but herding sheep. And for more than forty years the Apaches wandered, driving their sheep and cattle before them north in the summer and south in the winter.

Dulce, the only Jicarilla town, lies in a high meadow astride the highway from Chama to Farmington. A towering mesa juts up above the plain and even in summer the hint of the sternness of winter is evident. The Jicarilla home has a touch of fierce wilderness about it, befitting the Apache past.

In the 1940s oil men came and drilled a few holes in the Jicarilla land, and there came a roaring gusher. From being pauper poor, the Jicarillas suddenly became nouveau riche.

At first the Bureau of Indian Affairs handled all the money. And for a while it was doled out to individual Apaches, who had a tendency to go to Farmington or to Durango and blow it on junk.

But soon tribal leaders, running affairs from the BIA superintendent's office in Dulce, started taking an interest in ordering their own wealth. The tribal council, which was meeting quarterly, started meeting monthly.

On BIA advice the tribe at first plowed its investments into US Treasury bonds. And it established a $1 million education fund, enough to send every young Jicarilla through college—if he wanted to go.

The Apaches and Diversification

Eventually the Apache tribal council, quick learners in the world of finance, became dissatisfied with the status of their dividends and decided Government bonds didn't return a big enough investment. So it looked to diversify the portfolio.

The war whoop was "Invest in mutuals!" and "Buy blue chips!" And Charlie Vigil started quoting Dow Jones. Four New Mexico banks—the First National of Santa Fe, The Bank of New Mexico, the First National of Albuquerque, and the Albuquerque National—formed a combine to advise the Jicarillas on investments. They have developed a diversified portfolio.

And the Jicarilla constitution, rewritten in 1968, requires that the tribe invest no less than 15 percent of its income annually. That has come to about $350,000 a year. When the oil and gas run out, the Jicarillas will be as rich as ever—maybe richer.

The tribal leaders have tried to better the lot of the individual Jicarilla. They started a welfare program and make-work projects. Any Apache out of work can go down to the tribal woodyard now and get a job at $1.60 an hour.

The council wanted to see Dulce grow, so it began leasing out land to developers, who have built businesses and stores and subleased them to merchants. None of the businesses are Apache owned and the tribe doesn't want them to be. The Jicarillas are for integration. Says one, "We don't want this place to be too Apache."

The Jicarillas and Industry

For months the Jicarillas tried to lure industry onto the reservation to set up and employ Indians. It was the standard way to do things—BIA recommended. But the Jicarillas kept drawing a blank. The Zuñi reservation may be 40 miles from the nearest railroad. But the Apache is 80 miles.

The tribe interested two companies enough to send executives to take a look. The executives liked it, but their wives balked. They would have no part of isolation on a snowbound reservation surrounded by Apaches.

Thwarted, the Jicarillas decided to build their own industry and run it themselves. They built a $250,000 plant and now hire 160 Apaches, who make electronic assemblies for the F-106 aircraft, cooking pans for restaurants, and Sam Brown gun belts for the Los Angeles Police Department. . . .

So the tribe with the Midas touch is plowing ground as independent as their Zuñi brothers. They have proved themselves adroit financial manipulators. They hire expert professional help. . . .

Both tribes—the Zuñis and the Jicarilla Apaches—have won their independence from the white man by going two different ways. Although the BIA is still present at Dulce, Lawrence Kozlowski, the area superintendent, admits he is only a rubber stamp. He hasn't vetoed any Apache financial plan yet and doesn't expect to ever.

As pacesetters to Indian independence and self-determination both tribes are being watched by Indians across the United States. The prospect is for more tribes to be going their way.

VI. THE URBAN INDIANS

EDITOR'S INTRODUCTION

If the story of the Indian in his own setting is generally one of actual and hoped-for accomplishment (see Section V, above), the story of Indian integration into major metropolitan centers is a sordid and discouraging one. There are many instances—noted throughout this volume—of individual Indian achievement and adjustment to the "white man's world." But the fate of the reservation Indian seeking employment and a small measure of satisfaction and security in the city seems a doomed one, and strengthening of reservation life appears to be a much more desirable alternative. Can solutions be found to the integration of Indians into urban life? Should such solutions be sought and encouraged? Three articles deal with these questions.

Barbara Isenberg, member of the *Wall Street Journal* staff, lays out the discouraging facts. Michael Harris, writer on urban affairs for the San Francisco *Chronicle*, offers some suggestions for the Indian urban problems, and Leonard Chaebrowe, free-lance writer, asks whether it is all worthwhile—whether, in fact, it must be the Indians alone who will resolve the issue.

THE HARSH, UNFRIENDLY CITY [1]

Drunk, the stony-faced young Indian weaves up the stairs, dragging a faded blue windbreaker in one hand. His eyes focus dully on a sign on the top. It says, "Indians Discover America."

[1] From "Red Man's Plight: Urban Indians, Driven to Cities by Poverty, Find Harsh Existence," by Barbara Isenberg, staff reporter. *Wall Street Journal*. p. 1+. Mr. 9, '70. Reprinted with permission of *The Wall Street Journal* © 1970 Dow Jones & Company, Inc. All Rights Reserved.

His feet carry him up and into the Indian Welcome House. Framed in the doorway, he blurts out all he has come to say. "I'm done for, no damn good," he cries. "I don't care about nothin'!" Then he is gone, back to the alien streets of an alien city.

Every year thousands like him come to the nation's cities, driven there by privation on the Indian reservations. Often arriving with no job, no training, no prospects, only with the name of a relative and hope for a new life, the newcomer finds the metropolis almost as harsh as—and sometimes more so than—the place he left.

He suffers from massive culture shock; Afghanistan would be no more strange to many American Indians than Los Angeles. This contributes to an extraordinary rate of alcoholism that makes it all the harder for the migrant to keep and find a job. But still the Indians come.

According to social workers, cultural anthropologists and others, Indians already have formed an urban poverty-stricken group that ranks as one of the most oppressed and least understood of all. Talks with urban Indians reveal a growing bitterness against the white man and his ways and a growing militancy, recently exemplified by the Indian takeover of Alcatraz Island in San Francisco Bay and the growth of Indian organizations battling for Indian rights. . . .

The activist spirit seems certain to grow along with urban migration. . . . Many make their way to cities in the Midwest and West, such as Denver, Minneapolis and Los Angeles. The Indian population of Los Angeles alone has tripled in the past twenty years to some 60,000; as many as one of every eleven Indians in the United States is believed to live in this area, and more keep coming every day. . . .

If the city is so unkind, why do Indians keep coming? Migrants reply that the reservation is even worse. . . . Many Indians have been resettled in cities under relocation and job training programs of the Bureau of Indian Affairs. . . .

Critics maintain that BIA training programs are too heavily weighted toward manual skills in declining demand.

James Wilson, an Indian who is director of the Indian division of the Office of Economic Opportunity, says too many Indians are being trained in trades like welding, which is being shoved toward obsolescence by automation, and too few are being trained in white-collar skills. He claims three of every four urban Indians he has come in contact with are unemployed.

Many BIA-trained Indians are placed in jobs that have little or no relation to their training. The agency concedes that 22 percent of its trainees in fiscal 1969 "elected" to take such positions but says the rest were placed in jobs related to training.

Trudy Felix Brightman, an Indian in San Francisco, says the BIA brought her there for training as a dental technician, couldn't find her a job and finally sent her to work in a laundry as a clothes presser. Most of her friends, she says, left the dental training course only to wind up in factories. "That's one of the really criminal things the BIA does," argues a social worker familiar with Indian problems. "Bring somebody to the city, train him as a mechanic and then let him wind up doing something else."

Joe Vasquez, president of the Los Angeles Indian Center and a member of the city Human Rights Commission, declares: "After 180 years, the Indian is still unable to find his place in a white-dominated society. All the BIA does is manipulate our assets." Replies a BIA spokesman in Washington: "Obviously, we have shortcomings. We just don't have enough money to train everyone who might want to be trained, and it is hard for us to recruit people for our own agency and train them in the complexities of Indian problems."

But deficient as the existing BIA programs may be, they do at least offer urban migrants the hope of learning some skill and the chance of finding a job that will pay a survival wage. BIA says graduates of its urban programs in fiscal 1969 found employment that paid an average of $2.70 an hour for men and $1.93 for women. Also, Indians relocated and trained by BIA get a monthly stipend until they are placed.

That is more than most Indian migrants to the cities can expect when left to their own devices. Besides their lack of job skills, many also lack proficiency in English, making the search for work all the more difficult. Often they are joined in their wanderings by washouts from BIA relocation programs who are unable to find or keep jobs.

The result is an aimless drifting of Indians back to the reservations or from city to city. The BIA doesn't know the extent of these wanderings; it keeps no track of them, and it doesn't even keep current figures on how long the people it relocates stay in their jobs and cities. But a 1965 BIA study showed 40 percent of the relocated Indians returned to their reservations.

The total for migrants coming on their own is probably much higher. UCLA anthropologist Theodore Graves, who studied Indian newcomers to Denver, found that less than half stayed more than six months. Many went to other cities, and the rest returned to the reservation—only to find themselves equally ill-equipped to work there and with even less opportunity. For many Indians, this began a cycle of urban migration and return, each phase ending in fresh personal failure.

One of the first problems confronting many Indians making the transition from reservation to city life is the need to become familiar with the complexities of the modern world. Fred Connor, an Indian who came to Los Angeles five years ago, says he would bang on the back doors of buses, not understanding why they didn't open, and wander aimlessly through "the canyons whites call streets." In restaurants, he often found the menus incomprehensible.

But there are deeper-rooted problems. Anthropologists say that Indians are quick to share with fellow tribesmen whatever they have, place little importance on saving money for a rainy day and don't try to keep up with the Joneses.

In the city, they are thrust into a society that frowns on what whites would call "handouts," where thrift is a virtue and where fierce individual competition for jobs and status is the rule.

Indian time is one of sun and season, and the clock watching and stress on punctuality that whites display are puzzling to tribesmen. A woman civil service employee in one big Midwestern city recently was fired because she couldn't get used to going to work at a regular hour, and sometimes she didn't show up at all. In Minneapolis, the American Indian Movement often sends members to Indians' homes to drag workers out of bed and get them to the job.

For an appalling number of Indians, alcohol is preferable to accommodations to the white world. All too quickly, Indian migrants seem to find their way to the urban Indian bars—the Ritz in Los Angeles, the Larimer Street bars in Denver, the Shamrock or Sammy's Reservation in Chicago. Whites are unwelcome in most. A visitor to the Ritz, packed with Indians on a recent weekday morning, drew baleful stares.

Drunkenness is not an urban problem alone, of course. Drunken reservation Indians can be found on the streets of Gallup, New Mexico, the "Indian Capital of the World," any Saturday night—particularly since a judge ruled recently that the local house of detention couldn't take in more than sixty inebriates. It had been handling more than two hundred on weekend nights.

But the pressures of urban life in a strange society magnify alcoholism. No one knows the full extent of the problem, but all say it is enormous; a daytime walk through an Indian neighborhood in Los Angeles reveals many cases of drunkenness, and Indian leaders concede they are not isolated instances. "Many of our brightest people are in the bars," says Ernest Stevens, chairman of the California Inter-Tribal Council and himself a reformed alcoholic. "They know the truth, and they can't stand it."

THE NEW "RESERVATIONS" [2]

By now, Chicago has become one of the great Indian centers in the United States. So has Los Angeles, where one in every twenty Navajos, the largest tribe in the country, now lives. Like the Cherokees, who were forced by President Andrew Jackson to abandon their homes in the highland country of Georgia, North Carolina, and Tennessee and to march in great hardship along the "trail of tears" to far less lovely lands in Oklahoma, American Indians are moving today from poverty-stricken reservations to dreary city neighborhoods.

The trading off of rural hopelessness for despair in the city is evidence of the successes scored by recruiters from the Bureau of Indian Affairs on reservations in the Southwest, the Dakotas, and anywhere else Indians might be found, including Alaska. The Government agents promise jobs or education, decent housing, and a good life in the city. And then, after the prospects are persuaded to accept the offer, the recruiters issue one-way tickets to Minneapolis, Cleveland, Dallas, or any of several California cities that have imperceptibly become new camping grounds for American Indians.

Later, when the promised new job proves to be only part-time work at substandard wages, when the decent housing fails to materialize, and when the initial living allowance runs out, it is discovered that there are no guarantees to back up the golden promises. For many Indians, the move to the city means a shift from dependence on the Federal Government on the reservation to a place on the welfare rolls in the city. In financial terms, all that has happened has been the transfer of responsibility for part of the Indian population from the Bureau of Indian Affairs to local taxpayers.

[2] From "American Cities: The New Reservations," by Michael Harris, urban affairs writer, San Francisco *Chronicle*. *City*. 5:44-8. Mr.-Ap. '71. Reprinted by permission from *City*, Magazine of Urban Life and Environment, March-April 1971. Copyright 1971. The National Urban Coalition, 2100 M Street, N.W., Washington, D.C. 20037. All Rights Reserved.

Several years ago in Oakland, the Alameda County Department of Welfare was confronted with the problem of getting ten to twelve Indian families back to Alaska. "I told the Bureau of Indian Affairs, 'You brought them here, you take care of them,'" said Marguerite West, a section supervisor in the county welfare department. "But the Bureau said they have funds for bringing Indians here and no funds for returning them." The county finally paid the bill for repairing the error the Bureau of Indian Affairs had made when it shipped undereducated Alaskan families to the heart of a big city. Alameda County supplied the families with bus passage to Seattle and plane tickets for the rest of the trip home. . . .

The statistics are sketchy, and it can be said that the average Californian, like General George Armstrong Custer before him, has no idea how many Indians are in the vicinity. But the Indian population in California has almost surely passed the 100,000 mark, which means there are about as many Indians in the state today as there were before massacres, starvation, and disease during the days of the Gold Rush brought the population to a low of 16,000. The newcomers from out of state outnumber the native California Indians by a good margin. There are eighty-four reservations in the state, varying in size from two hundred square miles to small *rancherias* of a half-dozen or so families (or in one case, a bit of land occupied by a single Indian in San Diego County). Yet only about 10 percent of the Indian population in California occupies the reservation lands. . . .

Naturally there are some who survive the ordeal and who find their independence in the city or on the campus. There is evidence of a strong intellectual and artistic life in the quiet of the American Indian Historical Society in San Francisco or the more youthful, less settled atmosphere of the classes of Native American Studies on the Berkeley campus of the University of California.

Sometimes the new freedom is won not from the bureaucrats and other traditional enemies but from friends. In

1969 the last vestiges of white control were shaken from the Intertribal Friendship House in Oakland. White directors who had worked for the center for twelve years were voted out of office. "What have I done wrong?" one director asked, leaving the building in tears. "It was time for Indians to run their center themselves," an Indian leader explained.

Cities present an atmosphere in which Indians are inclined to put aside their tribal rivalries. There are a few tribal clubs, chiefly for the Sioux and Navajos, but a visitor to almost any Indian function in the San Francisco Bay Area—whether it is a party in the Berkeley hills or an appearance by a delegation in city hall or a meal on Alcatraz —finds a well-mixed assortment of Indians from many tribes. . . .

The concessions that cities make for Indians or any other newcomers are minimal. There is literally no one in City Hall charged—except in the most indirect, peripheral manner—with learning about the problems faced by San Francisco's Indians. Indeed, it took the invasion of Alcatraz [by activist Indians—Ed.] to make the city aware that the Indians existed.

The problem in cities, as many Indians see it, is that they are discouraged from being Indian. Indians watch black Americans being forcibly excluded from the main culture of the country and then see themselves being forcibly assimilated. . . .

Whether Indians are isolated physically, like the Cherokees in Oklahoma, or emotionally, like the Indians who pass almost unnoticed in the big cities, they need the chance for a better life. It is easy to list needs such as better education, housing, and economic opportunities, but how these things are to be accomplished is a complex and delicate matter. There is a great need for help from the larger society, but the answers will come from the Indians.

BACK TO THE RESERVATIONS? [3]

Over the last fifteen years the migration of American Indians into the cities has been headlong. At the same time the pace of the Indians' movement into the mainstream of urban life has been erratic, to a large extent deliberately so. For despite their migration, most Indians see their own culture as the equal of the white man's—technologically inferior, to be sure, but spiritually superior, or at any rate sovereign. Not that they are steadfast against assimilating. With half their population of about one million living away from the reservations and the Alaskan Native villages, such could hardly be the case. Only they aren't steadfast for assimilating either. Open to the possibility, they have approached warily, suspiciously, defensively, always remembering the life their people once knew.

The Indians are the only Americans with a dream of their own more American than the American Dream; a dream more impossible to realize, perhaps, because arising out of memory rather than a vision of the future, but for that reason more impelling. In their dream the streets, instead of being paved with gold, aren't paved at all. So they hesitate to exchange their remaining paths through the wilderness, paths offering them a communion both with nature and each other, for what is apparently only fool's gold.

The Indians' attachment to the past, to the pre-industrial past, strikes a responsive chord in urban Americans, one that is mainly sentimental but is sometimes more. There is a movement out of as well as into the urban mainstream, and many of the urban dropouts have at one point or another been inspired by Indian traditions. Yet it is easy to forget that the Indian pace is still two steps forward to modernization for every step in the opposite direction.

[3] From "Cross-Migrations," by Leonard Chabrowe, free-lance writer. *Columbia Forum.* 1:38-41. Summer '72. Excerpted from *The Columbia Forum*, Summer 1972, Vol. I, No. 3. © 1972 by the Trustees of Columbia University in the City of New York. Reprinted by permission.

In 1968, Stan Steiner, who long before had fled the streets of New York for a more natural landscape, published *The New Indians*, a book that paid homage to the tribes' resurgent pride in their traditions. Based mainly on interviews with the younger, more educated, and idealistic figures in what might be called the Indian Awakening, the book celebrated their determination to preserve the old communal values while overthrowing their colonial status and conditions. Not only would the new generation of Indians claim their rights as Americans to equality and prosperity, they would abide in the spirit of their forebears, who in closeness to the earth worshipped the forces of life rather than the power of money and machines.

Yet Steiner failed to speak to the younger, more educated, but pragmatic Indians to be found for the most part outside Indian territory. Individually stabilized in various currents of the mainstream, these other new Indians have been allowing their ties to the reservation and tradition to slacken. For them the dream of a free and innocent life in nature has faded before the reality of more immediate and individual needs. Among Indians generally, these pragmatists are few, but among educated Indians they are many, and probably signal more accurately than the idealists the direction in which Indians with greater options are inclined to go.

My own acquaintance with Indians began when, some time ago in Washington, I was hired as a writer by the Task Force on Racially Isolated Urban Indians, a group of seven American Indians being sponsored by the Government to work out the first housing, employment, and other social service programs for Indians in the cities. I'd had no experience in Indian affairs, only in the antipoverty program generally. And while I'd once read about the peaceful, restrained, agrarian Zuñis and the warlike, impassioned, maritime Kwackiutls, while I'd visited the Taos Pueblo and the Navaho reservation, I'd never troubled much about Indians. I'd simply assumed that sooner or later they would all be carried off by the urban mainstream or otherwise assimilated.

But in the course of my two-month stint I learned to see their situation from both the idealistic and pragmatic points of view. The two members of the Task Force with whom I traveled for three weeks—to Indian centers in Minneapolis, Los Angeles, Gallup and Fairbanks—embodied the pragmatic view.

One of them, a Creek-Seminole in his early thirties from Oklahoma, was then directing educational programs for Indians in Chicago. I will give him the name Donald McIver (the Creeks, both full and mixed bloods, often took their names from Scottish settlers for legal uses in the early years of the Republic). While at times afflicted with a stammer, Donald McIver didn't falter when he declared to me in the company of other Indians that he lacked the sense of Indianness so many of them proclaimed. In fact, he said he thought those who most loudly proclaimed it were only racists in reverse. No doubt what kept my companion from submerging himself in the communal Indian mystique, what made him skeptical that increasingly mobile Indians would continue to live by their old values, was his own personal striving in the society at large. But his skepticism also grew out of the findings of his University of Chicago Master's thesis, a sociological study of Indian life in Chicago. The study disclosed that those Indians who had fit into the mainstream culture—by virtue of their education and a middle-class income—tended to draw away from their ties of kinship and their attachment to the land. Education and higher living standards made urban individualists of Indians no less than of any other ethnic group.

Now a proponent of Indianness as a sovereign and viable culture might argue that Donald McIver's situation is exceptional. As a Creek-Seminole he belongs to the Five Civilized Tribes, which agreed several generations back to divide their Oklahoma territory into family properties, a step in keeping with the adaptability to white men's ways they'd already evinced before their removal from the Southeast in the 1830s. They'd become businessmen and slave-owning farmers, built homes and dressed in the white manner, embraced Christianity, and published a newspaper. In other words, my companion had grown up in a culture that had long since turned individualistic and placed a high value on education as a means of survival, a culture far removed from the typically Indian. But more to the point, no one is likely to feel an overriding racial identity without a communal home to return to. A people must either have land or, paradoxically, be persecuted in ghettos if its racial ties are to be maintained. How could the value placed by Indians on loyalty to the life of the tribe in nature apply where reservations, or reservation conditions, no longer exist? The indifference to Indianness of a Creek-Seminole is meaningless.

An answer to this argument, however, lies in the experience of my other companion, whom I will call Paul Sanchez (surnames of Spanish origin being common among Indians of the Southwest). As a Laguna Pueblo he belongs not only to a reservation tribe but to one with a centuries-old culture in one locale. With a master's degree from the University of Denver, backed up by several years as a social worker in two cities, he is now director of an Indian center in Minneapolis. Consequently, he takes only a passive interest in the affairs of his tribe in New Mexico. The urban current, together with his education and his marriage to a white girl, have carried Paul Sanchez away from the traditional life of the Lagunas.

What both my companions do feel is a strong family loyalty, a deep appreciation of their tribal heritage, and a persevering concern for the struggles of Indians. But each of them follows an independent personal path. They typify the growing number of Indians who, even if they have learned their own language first and English second, are now individuals first and Indians second.

Confused or mixed feelings about assimilation are nothing unusual. Virtually every ethnic minority in the United States has exhibited such feelings. Blacks, Jews, Italians, Mexicans, and Chinese, among others, have long exercised their instinct for group survival, for preserving their cultural identity, and not simply because they had little choice. Indeed, the melting pot has lately been overturned by the social ideal of cultural diversity. Nonetheless, the ethnic pride so often on display now is almost as often just display. Under the cover of different skin pigments, mother or grandmother tongues, religious and culinary habits, most minority Americans live like the majority, competitive and materialist, however much rebellious spirits would like it otherwise.

Cultural nationalism has its uses, of course. It is no mere frill of political fashion. Without it blacks might still feel compelled to lighten their skin, Jews to change their names, others to disguise themselves in ways equally debasing. In the endless struggle everyone must wage for self-esteem, minority citizens are no longer crippled simply by being different. But this does not mean there has been no assimilation, and assimilation where it counts—in the soul. For neither blacks nor any of the immigrant groups have resisted the call to become democratically mobile American status-seekers, industrial America's conspicuous consumers. Perhaps the very idea of resistance is gratuitous in this context, since none of the immigrant groups has come to America with a value system essentially opposed to competitive materialism. They have not resisted, because they've had no reason to—in their poverty and low estate, quite the contrary —and outside of preserving their cultural identity, they have actively sought assimilation.

To the Indians, though, assimilation is more threatening. Even more than their cultural identity, their ethos of communality in nature is at stake. To preserve that ethos they must resist, especially when poverty on the reservations makes the call of urban America all the more siren-like. Should the Indians be absorbed *in toto* by the cities, keeping a discernible identity or not, they would be prisoners of a civilization profoundly alien to theirs. In large measure they have already been prisoners for almost a century, but not where it counts.

While Indian resistance to assimilation is colored by much that is subjective, it has an objective source, a unique source among minority groups. The tribes still occupy a sizable portion of the continental USA—not counting Alaska, about 55 million acres or 86,000 square miles. Such an expanse is larger than most states and independent countries —large enough, for instance, to nourish a vigorous counterculture. And the recent Alaska settlement promises another 40 million acres.

What holds out hope for continued survival of the Indian ethos is that the reservation—despite its largely unarable land, its dirt-floor shanties, its patronizing Government officials, and its boredom—can never be as oppressive as the ghetto, simply because it is land. It is still open country owned by those who inhabit it. Whatever can be improved in city life, neither ghetto dwellers nor the well-to-do will gain relief from the fundamental urban conditions of congestion and concrete. The city, inner and outer, will always evoke a longing for nature.

Ironically, the call of the land is now having a negative effect on the Indians who have migrated into the cities, especially those migrants who have been drawn into ghettos. According to several studies, including Donald McIver's in Chicago, the reservation is what most deters Indians from coming to grips with city life. Unlike the great number of European immigrants who had nothing to go back to, Indians don't feel that they must succeed or else. The reservation is always there, offering a way out when adversity piles on.

With the reservation in mind Indians are tempted to say they don't want to be assimilated, they want only to be acculturated, which means taking what the whites have to offer and using it in their own way, enjoying the best of both worlds. Reasonable as this sounds, it frequently leads to giving up on the city entirely. Putting it another way, the reservation allows the Indian to hedge his bets. And the idea of acculturation, often a handy excuse for expected failure, in some measure promotes that failure. Many Indians are in perpetual motion between the reservation and the city. Instead of the best, they have the worst of both worlds. . . .

Not just Indians, of course, but many other Americans, especially white middle-class youths, are confused about where they are going. Swept along by the current of competitive materialism, they are simultaneously trying to move in other directions, often to create some form of communal life in a rural setting. These communalists have improvised reservations of their own and even sought to live among the Indians. Whether they have family money to draw on, sweat for their bread themselves, or wangle welfare, they like wearing headbands to keep their hair out of their eyes, Indian fashion. Traditional Indian life, including its transcendence-inducing religious practices, has become one of the models for an alternative to the competitive life. And the value placed by the counterculture on Indian traditions has in turn reinforced Indian nationalism. If Indianness thrives, it might be less because the Indians want it than because the palefaces need it.

Nobody, however, fully expects a revival of pure Indianness. Even those who most strive for it hope for no more than a balance. Both Indians and non-Indians are seeking to live in equal harmony with civilization and nature. Unfortunately, such a harmony is more easily seen than reached. At this stage of evolution it might no longer—or at best not yet—be possible. The era of industrial growth might simply be too competitive, too exploitative, for nature to hold its own. . . .

Yet if the forces of civilization and nature can be reconciled in a still expanding industrial age, the Indians just might reconcile them—or at least lead the way. For the reservations, protected under treaties with the Government, afford the tribes a better chance of finding a balance than any utopian groups in retreat from the cities. To the extent that the Indians sustain a secure and cooperative hold on their land, they will have a reinforcing physical tie to each other and to their traditional way of life.

In fact, should the Indians prosper materially and remain faithful in some measure to their tribal values, they might come to be considered as subversives undermining the Late Capitalist ethic of profit for the hell of it. Certainly they would be the proprietors of the most land and natural resources ever turned to communal—in effect, socialist—production in modern America. And thriving in a form of organization that bestowed full human benefits on all its members, they might even win the country back by assimilating, or at least acculturating, us.

VII. A CONFIDENT LOOK AHEAD

EDITOR'S INTRODUCTION

" 'The only good Indian' is a real Indian, not a white man with red skin."

Historian Carl Degler thus sums up the generally acknowledged view that in the future of the American Indian there will be much more stress on Indianness than on the historical American melting-pot theme (a theme now greatly suspect as a myth as it relates to many ethnic groups).

Where does the Indians' future lie? Those who comment on this topic in this final section adopt a confident air, but with uniform emphasis on the Indian way of life within America and perhaps on its value as a guide for our nation's future, especially as it relates to our increasingly serious struggle to learn or relearn how to live with our natural environment.

Another aspect of future trends is dealt with by Professor Hazel Hertzberg of Teachers College, Columbia University, who discusses pan-Indianism, the possible unity of various Indian cultures and ideals. Samuel Schonbach of the Los Angeles County Department of Parks and Recreation offers an idea from other lands—an ombudsman to protect and further Indian interests.

Vine Deloria, Jr., a Standing Rock Sioux, is a leading Indian spokesman. His books, articles, and speeches have been a major element in the current awareness of today's American Indian. In the selection printed here, Mr. Deloria goes all the way and raises the banner for the white man's adoption of "the total Indian way of life."

The final word in the section is free-lance writer Earl Shorris' poignant "Indian Love Call" with its message, admittedly a sad one, concerning the "life that was Indian."

INDIANS AND OTHER AMERICANS [1]

Vacillations in policy over the last century have stemmed largely from the refusal of white Americans to recognize that the Indians are not like other minorities, and particularly not like the blacks with whom they have so often been misleadingly compared. Over the years, it is true, individual Indians have left the reservations and made their way into the surrounding society. Others have done so selectively, working outside the reservation for a time and then returning to their people. But the striking fact is that whenever the Indians have been able to express their preferences either in words or "with their feet," they have made it clear that they do not want to be integrated into American society. As recently as 1952 over 60 percent of the Navajos—the largest single Indian group in the country—still did not speak English. Even among those tribes in which a much higher proportion speak English, it remains a second language. As the anthropologist Edward Spicer has pointed out in regard to the Indians of the Southwest under Spanish, American, and Mexican jurisdiction:

> At the end of 430 years, it was clear that, despite intensification of communication among all the peoples of the region, through the adoption of common language and a great deal of cultural borrowing and interchange, most of the conquered people had retained their own sense of identity. Moreover, there was little or no ground for predicting that even by the end of half a millennium of contact the native peoples would have ceased to exist as identifiable ethnic groups.

Nor has this refusal been principally a response to hostility from white society. Although there are and always have been undoubted acts of discrimination against Indians, white society has, on the whole, long been willing to accept Indians socially and economically to a degree that stands in

[1] From an article by Carl N. Degler, professor of history, Stanford University. Commentary. 54:68-72. N. 72. Reprinted from Commentary, by permission; copyright © 1972 by the American Jewish Committee.

marked contrast to its attitude toward blacks. Today a white person with Indian ancestry, for example, will readily admit to that ancestry—perhaps even with a certain amount of pride. Rare, however, is the white person who will own to any African ancestry, for to do so is to assume all the social and economic burdens that blackness incurs in American society.

There is a perverse irony in American practice toward Indians and blacks. America has offered to Indians what blacks have long wanted but been denied, while insisting upon for blacks what Indians have wanted but which blacks reject. Or, put another way, Indians have had the choice of becoming white men with red skins or remaining Indians. Generally speaking, blacks have enjoyed no such choice, even in theory, for from the time of slavery they have been forced to be a part of white culture. (The culture of the ghetto is at most a subculture and not comparable to the distinct Indian cultures even of today.)

Indians, when confronted with the choice, have chosen to be red men. This is why Indians, unlike blacks, do not demand civil equality. For to do so would be to acknowledge that they are an integral part of the white man's culture. Indians have consistently shown that they want to be treated as red men only.

It is just that insistence upon difference that has been so difficult for white Americans to accept. Immigrants and Negroes have insisted only upon individual acceptance and economic opportunity, and in theory, if not in practice, the dominant culture has found no difficulty in agreeing to these demands. The Indian demand for separate existence simply has no antecedent or analogy in the American experience. White native Americans, it is true, have known of other colored peoples at various times in the past who were judged incapable of becoming "white men"—Negroes, Chinese, and Japanese, for example. Never before, however, have white Americans encountered people who *refused* the opportunity to become Americans.

Perhaps because this refusal constitutes a blow to the national pride, white Americans have stubbornly continued to believe that Indians would eventually consent to become like them. Even a modern liberal organization like the Fund for the Republic has been unable to shake off the idea that the traditional approach to minorities in the United States must also be the proper one for Indians. On the opening page of the study *The Indian: America's Unfinished Business,* which the Fund financed and published in 1966, the goal was described as "making the Indian a self-respecting and useful American citizen. This policy involves restoring his pride of origin and faith in himself after years of crippling dependence on the Federal Government and arousing his desire to share in the advantages of modern civilization." Significantly, the last chapter of the study is devoted to "Policies Which Impede Indian Assimilation."

What are the implications for national policy of this recognition that Indians bear no real analogy to other social groups in the United States? The principal conclusion, it would seem, is to abandon the idea of making Indians over into white men with red skins. The right of *individual* Indians to leave the reservation and compete in the world outside should of course be retained. But it is time for other Americans to give up, once and for all, the expectation that somehow, in some way, at some time, the Indians in general will be absorbed into white society. The question should no longer be, "Why not the Indian?" but rather, "Why cannot the Indian remain an Indian?" Starting from where they are now, deciding their own future course of economic action, Indians ought to be helped to work out a way of life for themselves as separate communities within the larger American society.

If that policy can be carried out then the United States will have embarked upon an experiment in pluralism rare in the history of European expansion. Few modern governments have undertaken to protect and nurture a technologically weaker culture for the indefinite future. In America the basis of pluralism has been acceptance by the minority of the principal or central values of the society, with their differences from the majority remaining confined to relatively minor values or cultural traits. Thus Poles, or Irish Catholics, or Jews can be recognized as different in some habits and practices from the dominant culture, but at the same time the dominant culture assumes that each of the minorities will eventually learn English, participate in the standard occupations of the society, and live in a style that fits into an industrial and urban social order.

A special place for the Indian in American pluralism is justified by the fact that none of the forces or influences which have made assimilation an acceptable goal for other minorities are operative for him. Unlike any other minority, Indians did not come here voluntarily with a ready-made commitment to assimilation; unlike blacks, Indians have preferred to maintain a way of life distinct from the way of the whites.

A special place for Indians in American pluralism is justified, too, by the many treaties of recognition and support that white America so solemnly entered into with Indians over the years and then broke. For unlike any other social group in American history, Indians were promised support and encouragement in return for having given up their lands to European invaders. To accept Indianness as a social fact and as a part of American pluralism is but to acknowledge the debt that was incurred when one culture encountered another and pushed it aside. It is futile today to make a moral judgment of that epic clash of cultures; within the cultural context of the nineteenth century, let alone the seventeenth, that conflict does not seem to have been avoidable. Today, however, the Indians pose no threat, military or otherwise, to the dominant white culture. And certainly they no longer possess any large amounts of wealth that can further excite the cupidity of others.

In short, by recognizing what the past reveals to us about Indians and their culture, we are in a position to transcend our own history, and to recognize, in policy as well as in theory, that "the only good Indian" is a real Indian, not a white man with red skin.

PAN-INDIANISM [2]

Only a few decades ago most students of Indian affairs, together with many Indians, assumed that the Indian would eventually disappear as a distinct element in the American population. The assumption was shared by both those who regretted and those who welcomed its inevitability. This view has changed dramatically: it is now widely assumed that Indians will continue indefinitely as subgroups of the American people. If this latterday analysis is correct—and the evidence supporting it is formidable—Pan-Indianism seems likely not only to continue but to increase in importance.

Pan-Indian movements [the joining together of tribes for common action and life] in their modern accommodative form have represented a characteristic aspect of Indian relationships to the larger society and among each other throughout this century. Despite fluctuations in the significance and impact of particular types at particular periods, Pan-Indianism has shown itself to be remarkably durable, deeply rooted in Indian historical experience, and capable of considerable flexibility.

The forces which have helped to produce modern Pan-Indian movements are neither transient nor ephemeral. Some, like mass communications, urbanization, and education, are fundamentals of American life which will become more rather than less important in the future. Ideas travel fast. The "moccasin telegraph," the Indian version of the grapevine, still operates, and no doubt will continue to do so. But today Indians can and do get news and views directly from television and popular magazines, now found in many

[2] From *Search for an American Indian Identity*, by Hazel W. Hertzberg, associate professor of history and education, Teachers College, Columbia University. Syracuse University Press. 71. p 319-23. Copyright © 1971 by Syracuse University Press. Reprinted by permission.

an Indian home which even a decade ago was largely insulated from such immediate contact with the outside world. Automobiles and airplanes increase Indian mobility, enabling people with a long tradition of traveling to do so more rapidly, more frequently, and over longer distances. The national commitment to education is resulting in increasing numbers of young Indians going to colleges, including community colleges, where they imbibe new ideas not only in the classroom but probably more importantly from their peers, Indian and non-Indian. . . .

The sector of the Indian population from which Pan-Indian movements have historically risen will probably grow in size and importance. There can be little question that Indians will continue to leave the reservation, either permanently or temporarily, in significant numbers. Despite efforts to create viable reservation communities, the reservation base is unlikely to be sufficient to support its growing population. Some of these men and women will be lost in the general population but others will seek to retain or create an Indian identity. The immigrant experience is instructive in this regard. Even Americans separated by decades or centuries from their previous countries of origin are apt to refer to their previous "nationality," or "nationalities," since by this time they have often acquired several. Even those whose forebears came from places where there was little or no consciousness of an identity beyond locality or region have found it necessary and natural to create a "national" identity, the latest example being the renewed discovery of Africa by American blacks. Some form of "national" or ethnic identification, however vague, is thus so characteristic of the way Americans think about themselves that it seems highly likely that people whose homeland was reservation or tribe will continue to call themselves Indians, though they may not be readily identifiable either in appearance or life style as such. The Pan-Indian base will probably encompass not only Indians fresh from the reservation but also many who have lived in the larger society for generations.

Pan-Indianism will grow in local communities on or near reservations and in towns and cities as a result of increasing contacts among Indians and with whites. It will take a variety of forms from powwows to local and regional intertribal bodies. While these groups will have different degrees of tribal emphasis, they will of necessity assert a common Pan-Indian bond distinct from or complementary to tribal loyalties. This network of Pan-Indian ideas and activities will help to provide the kind of local base which national Pan-Indian movements have often lacked, and from which they may in the future arise.

The development of a Pan-Indian subculture, already noted by students of Indian affairs, may well satisfy the needs of Indians whose concerns are primarily local or fraternal. But today even fraternal Pan-Indianism engages in some national activities, as witness the annual "Miss Indian America" beauty contest which is supported by local Pan-Indian and local tribal groups. When Indians believe that they need to organize nationally, for whatever purposes, they will do so, supporting those national Pan-Indian organizations which exist or creating new ones to fulfill new functions. . . .

Pan-Indian movements will involve to some extent the reemergence of once-vanished Indians, or of persons whose Indian ancestry is exceedingly remote or even nonexistent. The more Pan-Indian the emphasis, the easier is such an occurrence, which is likely to be viewed with some skepticism by "real" Indians. Such skepticism will almost certainly be more pronounced in the case of Negroes who wish to participate in Pan-Indian movements. Some tribes have an admixture of Negro "blood," a circumstance which frequently causes considerable perturbation among other Indians. In some localities Negroes, whether or not they have or claim any Indian ancestry, participate in powwows and other fraternal activities. No doubt there is, and will be, a wide range of reactions among Indians; very little systematic study has yet been given to Indian views of Negroes. But it seems probable that Negro claims to be Indian will get a much cooler reception than similar white ones. People who view themselves as both different from the rest of society and as unfairly dealt with by it are usually notably unenthusiastic about confusion or fusion with groups whose social status is generally lower than their own. This is not of course to say that Pan-Indian movements will not advocate civil rights for all, or will not cooperate with black movements, or will not appropriate black tactics, but that they will do so in terms which make clear distinctions between the situation of Indians and the situation of Negroes. . . .

What specific varieties of Pan-Indian movements will arise in the future will depend to a very large extent on the climate of opinion, ideas, and styles of organization in American society as a whole. As in the past, Pan-Indian organizations will constitute not carbon copies but freehand versions of parallel organizations in the wider society, combining and adapting ideas, organizational forms, activities and definitions of the Indian drawn from both Indian and non-Indian sources. This process has been so fundamental in the development of Pan-Indianism as to make its continuation highly predictable.

AN OMBUDSMAN FOR INDIANS [3]

Although there have been put forth over the years many solutions stating what should be done to elevate the red man to a position of competence, none thus far has proved workable. Recently, however, Ake Sandler, a professor of government at Los Angeles State College, has offered a plan that promises to be as practical as it is good. His proposal is to establish a national ombudsman's post to protect the rights of the Indians. While a big part of an ombudsman's job is to investigate administrative acts which are contrary

[3] From "What the Red Man Needs," by Samuel Schonbach, Department of Parks and Recreation, Los Angeles County. *Catholic World*. 214:66-79. N. '71. Reprinted by permission of New Catholic World.

to law, he must also look into those which are "unreasonable, unfair, oppressive or discriminatory, even though in accordance with the law."

This protection would have as its ultimate purpose the goal of enabling the red man to manage his affairs and work out his own salvation. President Nixon recently expressed it thusly: "American Indians need federal cooperation rather than paternalism."

This goal would have little chance of success, however, without some means of guaranteeing the rights of the Indians. The ombudsman system proposed for this task makes use of independent and completely impartial officials. They work under a proven practice developed in the Scandinavian countries.

While three American states now have one ombudsman apiece, a single federal ombudsman could not handle all the complaints on the vast stage in Washington where the BIA is situated. Professor Sandler has offered a solution to the problem of how to apportion the work of his proposed federal ombudsman system. It would not be divided on a geographical basis, but first of all, among the divisions of government. Professor Sandler has also advocated having an ombudsman for each of the various minority groups, particularly the Indians because of their incomparable suffering. . . . How would a federal ombudsman remedy such discriminatory practices, since he can investigate, but has no enforcement powers? Herman S. Doi, ombudsman for Hawaii, said upon taking office in 1969, "My power will be in the reasonableness of my recommendations and the acceptance of them by the administrators."

It may be that Mr. Doi was somewhat modest, since the experience of Scandinavian countries has shown that bureaucrats there, including the police, fear nothing more than public exposure of their departments' abusiveness, incompetency or arrogance. After an ombudsman has screened out a justified complaint, he may use the press to publicly criticize (or "remind") an official at fault, but the criticism is always worded in such a way as to serve as information to other officials. Thus, patterns of administrative abuse can often be eliminated. Some years ago, the Danish ministry's faulty handling of mail was completely overhauled from the minister's office down to the mail room after the Danish ombudsman had publicized the complaints of two irate citizens from opposite ends of the nation.

But an ombudsman may report his findings officially to the chief executive and the legislature, as well as to the press. Thus, if attention is focused on discrimination against Indians in government health services, such conditions could ultimately be expected to be put under control across the entire United States.

However, the ombudsman's biggest job is to investigate the abuse of power by a bureaucracy. The worst pattern of BIA tyranny down through the years has stemmed from its methods of grabbing the red man's land. . . .

[As one example] the BIA may delay the payment of money legally due the Indians from leases, and the BIA superintendent, under certain conditions, can sign the lease on behalf of the owner without his permission. In Osage County, Oklahoma, when an Indian woman decided to move onto her land, she discovered that it had been leased for three years! The BIA had never even bothered to tell her, or to pass the rent on to her.

If this woman had had access to an ombudsman's office, she could have expected to receive prompt remuneration plus any damages incurred, because after an ombudsman decides in favor of an injured complainant, he always follows up by appointing a lawyer. She and her fellow tribesmen could have laughed and cheered, the way they often do in Scandinavia when the ombudsman publicizes his findings officially in favor of the citizenry. Furthermore, judging by Scandinavian experience, the BIA would soon lose its appetite for depriving innocent Indians of their land and possessions. . . .

Indians also suffer financially from the trading posts on their reservations, because the BIA does not properly supervise the practices of the monopoly it grants to the trader. A recent study by the Eureka *Times Standard* revealed that on the Navajo Reservation a can of coffee which costs the trader seventy-five cents, is resold to the Indian for $2.85! And interest rates charged by the post often go as high as 10 percent per month. . . .

Indian tribes are trying hard to advance in agriculture, and closely allied to this is the matter of water rights: one third of Indian land lies idle, largely for lack of irrigation. Water rights are one of the few Indian prerogatives laid out in clear judicial terms. The so-called Winters Doctrine spells this out unmistakably, but tribes have nevertheless often been swindled.

For the past few years, the Mojaves of California have been trying to regain their rights to the Colorado River. In 1967, the Mojaves did not even know until several months after the occurrence that hearings had been held and that the state had confiscated 1,500 acres of invaluable river frontage. California and the [United States] Interior department (in which the BIA is located) feared a water shortage and so reacted to pressure from the Metropolitan Water District of Southern California and private developers. The state laid claim to the area by citing the Swamp and Overflow Act of 1850 which allowed river swampland to be placed under state jurisdiction. This claim was shown to be fraudulent by private hydrologists who proved the acreage claimed was clearly too high to have ever been a swamp, and that it was never even part of the original river bed when the law was enacted in 1850.

A great deal needs to be done for Indian education. Its failure can be shown by the fact that the dropout rates among them are twice the national average, and that Indian children score consistently lower than white children at every grade level. In areas now where Indian schools are scarce, the BIA sends children to boarding schools many miles away from their parents. This condition could be alleviated if BIA funds were more carefully disbursed. One example of the misuse of funds was shown by the Indian Education Subcommittee Hearings in Congress in 1967, revealing that money appropriated for Indian education was being siphoned off for white schools. Even in BIA day-schools, the Indians must often travel long distances by bus, where the child is deliberately kept in ignorance of his culture, history and heritage.

Indian children also suffer severe discrimination in public schools. In Ponca City, Oklahoma, it was discovered that a teacher accommodated the feelings of her white pupils by permitting them to sit separately from Indian children.

An Indian student in a public school in the state of Washington objected to the American history textbook that called her ancestors "dirty savages." She was soon expelled for being "uncontrollable," and the mother was forced to send her daughter hundreds of miles to an Indian boarding school in Oklahoma.

Many Indian tribes are fighting for their own schools as one step toward cultural survival. Thus far, however, there has been only one reservation which has been able to demonstrate how this policy would work. The Navajo Reservation —largest in the nation—is about the size of West Virginia and reaches into portions of Arizona, New Mexico, Utah and Colorado. The Navajos still have much misery in their midst, but their economic condition is generally better than that of other tribes. So, in July 1966, the Rough Rock School, a private, nonprofit organization, was established on the Navajo Reservation in Chinile, Arizona. Its first director, Robert A. Roesscl, Jr., declared, "The Indians ought to be able to be Americans and Indians, too."

The school uses Navajo teachers and teachers' aides in the classroom, and it employs bilingual instruction and course material reflecting the richness of the Navajo culture. Equally important, it carries on extensive community and parental participation in school affairs. Director Roessel's goal thus appears to be working out.

Encouraged by these results, the tribe, in January 1969, opened the Navajo Community College at Many Farms, Arizona. The tribal leaders had obtained a $475,000 grant from the Government and $60,000 from the William H. Donner Foundation. To this they added $200,000 more from tribal funds to start the Community College in a borrowed building.

On opening day, trim coeds and young men in tight Levis and cowboy boots were there. They mingled with old women in velveteen skirts and with old men in shabby clothes and tall, black, felt hats. The tribal elders were on hand because they wanted to learn the history of their Navajo ancestors. Some of the young students wanted to learn a trade, but many wanted further academic study toward a degree at a four-year college. Yet, regardless of their purpose, all had a particular pride in the first institution of higher learning on any Indian reservation in the country.

Many other tribes are now hoping for their own Indian-controlled schools, but to make this the rule rather than the exception, these tribes must first bolster their economy so that they can afford such schools. This, in turn, depends upon them asserting their rights as American citizens.

An ombudsman, protecting their rights, would be best qualified to help these tribes realize their dream. While he has no enforcement powers, his authority to subpoena records and witnesses, plus his official practice of publicizing and exposing the wrong-doing of Government agencies would be a powerful weapon for the Indians in their fight for economic justice.

In the important field of education, the ombudsman could be of great benefit in reform. He not only handles complaints; his chief value in bringing about improvements lies in his practice of making annual inspection tours with the aid of his staff to all types of Government agencies, schools and institutions. His reports and recommendations are then closely studied by the legislature.

Former presidential advisor, Clark Mollenhoff, recently declared, "The creation of the post of national ombudsman would do more to restore citizens' faith in the Federal Government than any other single act."

A national ombudsman for the Indians would do even more for the red men. It would help them to restore faith in *themselves*.

FOR SURVIVAL—THE INDIAN WAY [4]

In recent years we have come to understand what progress is. It is the total replacement of nature by an artificial technology. Progress is the absolute destruction of the real world in favor of a technology that creates a comfortable way of life for a few fortunately situated people. Within our lifetime the difference between the Indian use of land and the white use of land will become crystal clear. The Indian lived with his land. *The white destroyed his land. He destroyed the planet earth.*

Non-Indians have recently come to realize that the natural world supports the artificial world of which they are so fond. Destruction of nature will result in total extinction of the human race. There is a limit beyond which man cannot go in reorganizing the land to suit his own needs. . . .

We can be relatively certain that the federal and state governments will not take an objective view of land use. Agencies established to protect the public interest are subject to heavy political pressure to allow land to slip away from their trusteeship for short-sighted gains by interest groups. . . . The American public is totally unconcerned about the destruction of the land base. It still believes in the infallibility of its science, technology, and Government.

[4] From *We Talk, You Listen*, by Vine Deloria, Jr., Standing Rock Sioux, former executive director, National Congress of American Indians. Macmillan. '70. p 186-90, 195-7. Reprinted with permission of Macmillan Publishing Co., Inc. from *We Talk, You Listen* by Vine Deloria, Jr. Copyright © 1970 by Vine Deloria, Jr.

Sporadic and symbolic efforts will receive great publicity as the future Administrations carefully avoid the issue of land destruction. Indian people will find their lands under continual attack and will probably lose most of them because of the strongly held belief that progress is inevitable and good.

With the justification of progress supporting the destruction of Indian tribes and lands, the question of results becomes important. Four hundred years of lies, cheating, and genocide were necessary in order for American society to destroy the whole planet. The United States Government is thus left without even the flimsiest excuse for what has happened to Indian people, since the net result of its machinations is to destroy the atmosphere, thus suffocating mankind.

There is a grim humor in the situation. People used to make fun of Indians because of their reverence for the different forms of life. In our lifetime we may very well revert to panicked superstition and piously worship the plankton of the sea, begging it to produce oxygen so that we can breathe. We may well initiate blood sacrifices to trees, searching for a way to make them productive again. In our lifetime, society as a whole will probably curse the day that white men landed on this continent, because it will all ultimately end in nothingness.

Meanwhile, American society could save itself by listening to tribal people. While this would take a radical reorientation of concepts and values, it would be well worth the effort. The land-use philosophy of Indians is so utterly simple that it seems stupid to repeat it: man must live with other forms of life on the land and not destroy it. The implications of this philosophy are very far-reaching for the contemporary political and economic system. Reorientation would mean that public interest, indeed the interest in the survival of humanity as a species, must take precedence over special economic interests. In some areas the present policies would have to be completely overturned, causing great political dislocations in the power structure. . . .

For years Indian people have sat and listened to speeches by non-Indians that gave glowing accounts of how good the country is now that it is developed. We have listened to people piously tell us that we must drop everything Indian as it is impossible for Indians to maintain their life style in a modern civilized world. We have watched as land was stolen so that giant dams and factories could be built. Every time we have objected to the use of land as a commodity, we have been told that progress is necessary to the American way of life.

Now the laugh is ours. After four centuries of gleeful rape, the white man stands a mere generation away from extinguishing life on this planet. Granted that Indians will also be destroyed—it is not because we did not realize what was happening. It is not because we did not fight back. And it is not because we refused to speak. We have carried our responsibilities well. If people do not choose to listen and instead overwhelm us, then they must bear the ultimate responsibility.

What is the ultimate irony is that the white man must drop his dollar-chasing civilization and return to a simple, tribal, game-hunting, berry-picking life if he is to survive. He must quickly adopt not just the contemporary Indian world view but the ancient Indian world view to survive. He must give up the concept of the earth as a divisible land area that he can market. The lands of the United States must be returned to public ownership and turned into wilderness if man is to live. It will soon be apparent that one man cannot fence off certain areas and do with the land what he will. Such activity will be considered too dangerous to society. Small animals and plants will soon have an equal and perhaps a greater value for human life than humans themselves.

Such a program is, of course, impossible under the American economic and political system at the present time. It

would interfere with vested economic interests whose motto
has always been "the public be damned." Government policy
will continue to advocate cultural oppression against Indian
tribes, thinking that the white way of life is best. . . . [In
1969] five powerful Government agencies fought the tiny
Lummi tribe of western Washington to prevent it from developing a bay that the tribe owned as a sealife sanctuary.
The agencies wanted to build massive projects for commercial
use on the bay, the Indians wanted it developed as a conservation area restoring its original food-producing species
such as fish, clams, and oysters. Fortunately, the tribe won
the fight, much to the chagrin of the Army Corps of Engi-
neers, which makes a specialty of destroying Indian lands.

The white man's conception of nature can be characterized as obscene, but that does not even begin to describe it.
It is totally artificial and the very existence of the Astrodome
with its artificial grass symbolizes better than words the
world visualized by the non-Indian. In any world there is
an aspect of violence that cannot be avoided; Nature is ar-
bitrary and men must adjust to her whims. The white man
has tried to make Nature adjust to his whims by creating
the artificial world of the city. But even here he has failed.
Politicians now speak reverently of corridors of safety in the
urban areas. They are main lines of transportation where
your chance of being robbed or mugged are greatly reduced.
Everywhere else there is indiscriminate violence. Urban man
has produced even an artificial jungle, where only the fittest
or luckiest survive.

With the rising crime rate, even these corridors of safety
will disappear. People will only be able to go about in the
urban areas in gangs, tribes if you will. Yet the whole situation will be artificial from start to finish. The ultimate conclusion of American society will be that even with respect
to personal safety it was much safer and more humane when
Indians controlled the whole continent. The only answer
will be to adopt Indian ways to survive. For the white man

even to exist, he must adopt a total Indian way of life. That is really what he had to do when he came to this land. It is what he will have to do before he leaves it once again.

INDIAN LOVE CALL [5]

The time of islands is over. Insularity is now the province of madmen and doomed societies. Man, the tool maker, is being made over by his tools. And the tools are inflexible; men must adapt themselves to them. The Indian, being human, wants, and to satisfy those wants he must sacrifice himself to the tools that provide them. It is not an easy sacrifice, for it is one's uniqueness that is devoured by the machine, and the Indian is thrashing about in his soul to find a different bargain with the twentieth century.

There is no other bargain to be made. On a crowded earth one surrenders to the machines or perishes. The ripening of chokecherries and the coming of thunder are unacceptable marks of time for the machine. A language that exists in the context of the moment is not suited to the exploration of new planets. And what Indian can fail to know? The machine tells everyone everything instantaneously, without regard for truth, innocent of its own power.

In this last effort to remain an island, the Indian is a man aware of his dying. He gasps, his nerves convulse, he calls himself an activist, radical, traditionalist, Native American, possessor by right of discovery, and he is dying, slipping over into the next world of faceless, machinebound existence while his tiring heart hangs in the previous world, hoping for a miracle from Wakan-tanka, Manitou, Taiowa. Any miracle from any quarter will do.

As an Indian, he is an object of the white man's creation, bearing the white man's name, living in the white man's boundaries, watching himself in movies recreated according to the white man's version. The museum, the zoo of the dead,

[5] A chapter from *Death of the Great Spirit*, by Earl Shorris, free-lance writer. Simon & Schuster. '71. p 250-3. Copyright © 1971 by Earl Shorris. Reprinted by permission of Simon & Schuster.

awaits him. As a bicultural man, he is usually a schizo-
phrenic transition, the object and the enemy of himself, one
organism containing two foreign bodies, an endless process
of rejection. There is only the melting pot, and after that
process what will he be? Will he fare any worse than the
rest of us?

It is the process that is killing. Those who fight hardest,
the activists, are the ones who suffer most, prolonging in
themselves the death agonies, confusedly seeking succor in a
world that ceased to exist before they were born. The suffering produces the anger they turn against each other and
against all Indians. A man who seeks to save Indian traditions, who claims to glory in them, makes jokes about "Indian time." An activist says confidentially, "Don't believe
everything Indians tell you; Indians don't tell the truth." It
does not occur to him that he has given a paradox for advice;
in his frustration he has come to believe it.

At the Cook Christian Training School in Tempe, Arizona, Ernest Bighorn teaches Indian culture. He has learned
the culture from books and from tape-recorded interviews
with other Indians. If it has occurred to him that Christianity is not an Indian religion, he does not talk about it.

Conquered and loved, butchered and smothered, the Indian staggers into the battle for a pluralistic society; he has
seen death in the melting pot. Hank Adams, born at Poverty
Flat, Fort Peck Indian Reservation, raised on the Quinnalt
Reservation in Washington, chain-smokes filter-tip cigar-
ettes, punctuating the inhalations with sips of coffee and
painfully composed sentences: "All the people I grew up
with have either been killed or they killed themselves." He
talks about the late Senator [Robert] Kennedy who gave his
telephone credit card to the Indians who went to the Poor
People's March so they would feel less lonely. His is another
premature death in Hank Adams' life. There is an aura of
that fate about him. He seems to have lived beyond his time,

and he is not yet thirty years old. "When I say develop a
new Indian life," he confesses, "it doesn't mean the life of a
hundred years ago, or a thousand years ago. I'm not certain
what it means."

A pluralistic society in the time of television? An Apache
girl said she used to cheer for the soldiers when she saw
movies about Indians on television. Juana Lyon, who calls
herself an activist, refused to tell the name of her grand-
father, because "he's always referred to as the chief of the
most savage, bloodthirsty group of Indians." She was probably talking about Quanah Parker, who fought the hunters
who came into Comanche lands, and later held his tribe together during the first traumatic years of reservation life.
The functional history is whatever is believed about the past,
and Indians are not excepted from the recreating of history
in an electrified tube. They are beset with the same information and misinformation as the rest of us. How can they not
respond as we do?

The success of the lovers is assured by the machinery of
the society of lovers; the Indian is arriving at the point where
the lovers may have complete empathy with him. He can
then be freed from hunger and disease, for he will have become human, recreated at last wholly in the image of his
conquerors.

There was a life that was Indian, and though it has been
made dead by the freezing eye of the anthropologist and the
honeyed hand of the reformer, Indians cannot let go the
memory of it. In this lost life they see their power. They call
for a renaissance.

And what is raised up from the past? A girl of ten, perhaps twelve, years steps onto a cement platform. She is
dressed in bucksin and beads. Beside her is a canvas tipi. Her
dance will open a three-day Intertribal Powwow at Hayward,
California. It is a gathering of Indians, a pageant for the old
way, a feast of identity. The girl assumes a position defined

by Pierre Beauchamp for the Paris Opera, and begins to dance to a recording of Nelson Eddy and Jeanette Mac-Donald singing "Indian Love Call."

> Indians! There are no Indians left now but me.
> Sitting Bull 1844(?) —1890

BIBLIOGRAPHY

An asterisk (*) preceding a reference indicates that the article or a part of it has been reprinted in this book.

BOOKS, PAMPHLETS, AND DOCUMENTS

Bahr, H. M. and others, eds. Native Americans today: sociological perspectives. Harper. '71.

Brown, D. A. Bury my heart at Wounded Knee; an Indian history of the American West. Holt. '71; paper ed. Bantam. '72.

Bryde, J. F. The Indian student: a study of scholastic failure and personality conflict. 2d ed. University of South Dakota Press. '70.
> Bibliography p 97-109.

Cahn, E. S. ed. Our brother's keeper: the Indian in white America. New Community Press, Inc. 3210 Grace St. N.W. Washington, D.C. 20007. '70. [for sale by World Publishing Company]

Commission on the Rights, Liberties, and Responsibilities of the American Indian. The Indian: America's unfinished business; report comp. by W. A. Brophy and S. D. Aberle. University of Oklahoma Press. '66.

Debo, Angie. A history of the Indians of the United States. University of Oklahoma Press. '70.
> Bibliography p 359-63.

Deloria, Vine, Jr. Custer died for your sins: an Indian manifesto. Macmillan. '69; paper ed. Avon Books. '70.

*Deloria, Vine, Jr. We talk, you listen; new tribes, new turf. Macmillan. '70.

Driver, H. E. Indians of North America. 2d ed. rev. University of Chicago Press. '69.
> Bibliography, p 567-93.

Feder, Norman. American Indian art. Abrams. '69.

Feder, Norman. Two hundred years of North American Indian art. Praeger. '72.

*Hertzberg, H. W. Search for an American-Indian identity; modern Pan-Indian movements. Syracuse University Press. '71.

Index to literature on the American Indian, 1970. Indian Historian Press, Inc. 1451 Masonic Av. San Francisco, Calif. 94117. '72.

*Indian voices; the first convocation of American Indian scholars. Indian Historian Press, Inc. 1451 Masonic Av. San Francisco, Calif. 94117. '70.
    Reprinted in this book: "Moment of truth for the American Indian," by Rupert Costo. p 3-8; "Red power, real or potential," by Beatrice Medicine. p 299-307.

Jones, L. T. Amerindian education. Naylor. '72.

Jones, L. T. Indians at work and play. Naylor. '71.

Josephy, A. M. The Indian heritage of America. Knopf. '68; paper ed. Bantam. '69.

*Josephy, A. M. comp. Red power: the American Indians' fight for freedom. American Heritage Press. '71.

Klein, Bernard, and Icolari, Daniel. Reference encyclopedia of the American Indian. Klein. '67.

Levine, Stuart, and Lurie, N. O. eds. The American Indian today. Edwards, Everett. '68; rev. ed. Penguin Books. '70.

Levitan, S. A. and Hetrick, Barbara. Big brother's Indian programs, with reservations. McGraw-Hill. '71.

Locke, R. F. ed. The American Indian. Mankind Publishing Co. 8060 Melrose Av. Los Angeles, Calif. 90046. '70.

Meyer, William. Native Americans: the new Indian resistance. International Publishers. '71.

Museum of the American Indian. Books about Indians. The Museum. Broadway at 155th St. New York 10032. '72.

Neils, E. M. Reservation to city: Indian migration and federal relocation. (Research paper no 131) University of Chicago. Department of Geography. '71.
    Bibliography, p 195-8.

*Nixon, R. M. Recommendations for Indian policy; message from the President of the United States transmitting recommendations for Indian policy. (House. Document no 91-363) 91st Congress, 2d session. Supt. of Docs. Washington, D.C. 20402. '70.

Schlesier, K. H. The Indians of the United States; an essay on cultural resistance. (Bulletin, v 45, no 4; University studies, no 81) Wichita State University. 1845 Fairmount. Wichita, Kans. 67208. '69.

Schusky, E. L. The right to be Indian. Indian Historian Press, Inc. 1451 Masonic Av. San Francisco, Calif. 94117. '70.

*Shorris, Earl. Death of the great spirit; an elegy for the American Indian. Simon & Schuster. '71.
   Excerpt: How 114 washing machines came to the Crow reservation. Atlantic. 227:3-7. F. '71.

Sorkin, A. L. American Indians and federal aid. Brookings. '71.

Steiner, Stanley. The new Indians. Harper. '68.
   Bibliography. p 327-36.

Terrell, J. U. American Indian almanac. World Publishing. '71.
   Bibliography, p 455-66.

United States. Commission on Civil Rights. American Indian civil rights handbook. (Clearinghouse publication no 33) '72. The Commission. 1121 Vermont Av. N.W. Washington, D.C. 20425.

United States. Congress. Joint Economic Committee. Subcommittee on Economy in Government. Toward economic development for native American communities; a compendium of papers. (91st Congress, 1st session). Supt. of Docs. Washington, D.C. 20402. '69. 2v.

United States. Congress. Senate. Committee on Interior and Insular Affairs. Policy changes in the Bureau of Indian Affairs. (91st Congress, 2nd session) Supt. of Docs. Washington, D.C. 20402. '70.

United States. Department of the Interior. Bureau of Indian Affairs. Answers to your questions about American Indians. Supt. of Docs. Washington, D.C. 20402. '70.

*United States. Department of the Interior. Bureau of Indian Affairs. Information about the Bureau of Indian Affairs. Supt. of Docs. Washington, D.C. 20402. [mimeographed] '71.

United States. Department of the Interior. Bureau of Indian Affairs. Publications pricelist [of the] Bureau of Indian Affairs. Haskell Indian Junior College. Lawrence, Kans. '73.

United States. Department of the Interior. Bureau of Indian Affairs. Office of Education Programs. Fiscal year 1972 statistics concerning Indian education. Haskell Indian Junior College. Lawrence, Kans. '71.

United States. Government Printing Office. Public Documents Department. Smithsonian Institution national museum and Indians. (Price list 55, 43d ed.) The Department. Washington, D.C. 20402. '72. p 1-5.

United States. National Council on Indian Opportunity. Report. The Council. 726 Jackson Pl. N.W. Washington, D.C. 20506. '70.

Waddell, J. O. and Watson, O. M. eds. The American Indian in urban society. Little. '71.

*Washburn, W. E. Red man's land/white man's law. Scribner. '71.

*Wax, M. L. Indian Americans: unity and diversity. Prentice-Hall. '71.

Wise, J. C. Red man in the new world drama. Macmillan. '71.

Woods, R. G. and Harkins, A. M. Examination of the 1968-69 urban Indian hearings held by the National Council on Indian Opportunity. University of Minnesota. Center for Urban and Regional Affairs. Minneapolis, Minn. 55455. '71.

PERIODICALS

America. 122:465-7. My. 2, '70. Lords of the rock: occupied Alcatraz. J. A. Coleman.

America. 127:445. N. 25, '72. Can Indians trust Washington. J. F. Donnelly.

American Anthropologist. 72:9-34. F. '70. Navajo filmmakers. Sol Worth and John Adair.

American Anthropologist. 72:35-54. F. '70. Personal adjustment of Navajo Indian migrants to Denver, Colorado. T. D. Graves.

American Anthropologist. 72:90-7. F. '70. Northern Iroquoian sociopolitical organization. Elisabeth Tooker.

American Anthropologist. 74:1180-8. O. '72. Indian culture and industrialization. R. H. Bigart.

*American Heritage. 24:49-55. F. '73. Hopi way. A. M. Josephy, Jr.

American Journal of Public Health. 60:1769-87. S. '70. Alcoholism, illness, and social pathology among American Indians in transition.

American Libraries. 4:115-17. F. '73. Selected bibliography of bibliographies of Indian materials for adults.

American West. 6:52-3. Ja. '69. Red power. W. E. Washburn.

American West. 10:34-9+. Ja. '73. Senator's happy thought: J. G. Fair's idea to use Santa Catalina Island as an Apache reservation. J. E. Baur.

American West. 10:4-9. Mr. '73. Indian agent: a study in corruption and avarice. Langdon Sully.

Arizona Business Bulletin. 17:12-72. D. '70. Reservation Indian and mainstream economic life. B. J. Taylor.

Black Politician. 1:37-9. Fall '69. Red power. Lehman Brightman.

*Bulletin (Dartmouth College). 52 (no 9):1-4. Je. 30, '72. [Report of the Indian symbol study committee; R. D. Kilmarx, chairman.]

Business Week. p 118-20. Je. 7, '69. American Indians come nearer mainstream.

Business Week. p 72-3. Ap. 4, '70. Industry invades the reservation.

California Law Review. 58:445-90. Mr. '70. Indian battle for self-determination. Robert Ericson and D. R. Snow.

*Catholic World. 214:66-70. N. '71. What the red man needs. Samuel Schonbach.

Choice. 6:1709-19. F. '70. North American Indians: 1492-1969. A. H. Whiteford.

Christian Century. 87:1103-5. S. 16, '70. Lutherans and American Indians: a confrontation. E. R. Trexler.

Christian Century. 88:65-8. Ja. 20, '71. America's most oppressed minority. H. E. Fey.

*Christian Century. 89:208-10, 225-6. F. 16-23, '72. Indian resources. Pat Porter.

Christian Century. 90:356-7. Mr. '73. Wounded Knee: a struggle for self-determination. Ted Elbert.

*Christian Science Monitor. p 1+. Ja. 2; 1+. Ja. 4; 9. Ja. 7; 9. Ja. 8; 9. Ja. 9, '71. Decade of the Indian. Jack Waugh.

Christian Science Monitor. p 17. Ap. 8, '71. Happiness is seeing red—to Grace Thorpe. J. A. Levine.

*City. 5:45-8. Mr.-Ap. '71. American cities: the new reservations. Michael Harris.

Civil Rights Digest. 3:9-15. Summer '70. Tribal sovereignty and the 1968 Indian bill of rights. Michael Smith.

*Columbia Forum. 1:38-41. Summer '72. Cross-migrations. Leonard Chabrowe.

*Commentary. 54:68-72. N. '72. Indians and other Americans. C. N. Degler.

Commonweal. 92:432-6. S. 4, '70. Nixon and the Indian. Rennard Strickland and Jack Gregory.

Community. 46:6-9+. Mr.-Ap. '71. American Indian: minority or minorities. Daniel Langdon.

*Congressional Record. 119:S11414-16. Je. 19, '73. Indian economic development and employment act of 1973. George McGovern.

Ebony. 26:70-2+. D. '70. Red and black: the Indians and the Africans. Lerone Bennett, Jr.

Economist. 236:41-2. Jl. 18, '70. First Americans last again?

Economist. 242:45. Ja. 15, '72. Aim for red power.

Economist. 245:55. N. 18, '72. More Indian wars.

Editorial Research Reports. v2 no 18:847-68. N. 8, '72. Preservation of Indian culture. R. C. Schroeder.

English Journal. 62:37-41. Ja. '73. Literature of the American Indian. Peter Dillingham.

Esquire. 74:107-9+. Ag. '70. New Indian. Roy Bongartz.

Esquire. 74:162-7+. N. '70. Soul of the Navajo. Jules Loh.

Ford Foundation Letter. 2:2-3. D. 1, '71. American Indian—beyond survival. Oona Sullivan.

Good Housekeeping. 172:78-9+. Ja. '71. America's oldest debt: justice for the Indians. J. N. Bell.

Harper's Magazine. 241:81-4. O. '70. Man called Perry Horse. John Corry.

Harper's Magazine. 245:79-84. Ja. '73; 22+. Mr. '73. Indian giving. Eric Treisman.

Harper's Magazine. 246:46-8+. Je. '73. Bamboozle me not at Wounded Knee. Terri Schultz.

Human Organization. 29:155-61. Fall '70. Self-help at Fort Yuma: a critique. R. L. Bee.

Human Organization 31:112-240. Summer '72. Modernization research on the Papago Indians. R. A. Hackenberg and others.

Human Organization. 31:257-70. Fall '72. Menominee termination: from reservation to colony. N. O. Lurie.

Indian Truth. 48:13-14. Ap. '71.
    Periodical published by Indian Rights Association, 1505 Race St. Philadelphia, Pa. Lists current available paperbacks about American Indians.

*Industry Week. 171:14-17. O. 18, '71. Firms find Indian reservation is good place to locate plant.

Industry Week. 173:22-3. Ap. 24, '72. Indian reservations prove good plant sites.

Intellect. 101:208-9. Ja. '73. Higher education for Indians and Spanish-speaking Americans; Ford Foundation grants.

Intellectual Digest. 3:44-6. O. '72. Indian past. John Bierhorst, ed.

Intellectual Digest. 3:47-50. O. '72. Indian present. Fritz Scholder and R. H. Turk.

*International Journal of Comparative Sociology. 11:58-66. Mr. '70. Indian dilemma. E. L. Schusky.

Interplay. 3:20-4. Ag./S. '69. Not-so-vanishing American. N. S. Hey.

Johns Hopkins Magazine. 23:23-7. Spring '72. Poorest nonwhite minority. J. C. Schmidt.

Journal of Negro Education. 38:242-6. Summer '69. The American Indian (a stifled minority). W. B. Welch.

Journal of the West. 9:93-109. Ja. '70. Land tenure and economic development on the Warm Springs Indian reservation. Jack Hunt.

Journal of the West. 10:521-34. Jl. '71. Wheeler-Howard Act of 1934: the Indian New Deal. M. T. Smith.

Library Journal. 95:463-7. F. 1, '70. A wind is rising; Navajo community college. B. E. Richardson.

Library Journal. 96:2848-51. S. 15, '71. Plight of the native American. Rey Mickinock.

Life. 71:5, 38-47. Jl. 2, '71. Our Indian heritage [with editorial comment].

Life. 71:48-52+. Jl. 2, '71. Custer myth. A. M. Josephy, Jr.

Life. 71:60-5. Jl. 2, '71. Surprising riches of Indian art.

Look. 34:23-34. Je. 2, '70. America's Indians. William Hedgepeth.

Mademoiselle. 72:202-4+. Ap. '71. American thing: white society is breaking down around us [interview, ed. by Peter Collier]. Vine Deloria, Jr.

Mental Hygiene. 55:174-7. Ap. '71. Extent and significance of suicide among American Indians today. R. J. Havighurst.

Mental Hygiene. 55:199-205. Ap. '71. Cultural conflict in urban Indians. Joan Ablon.

Midcontinent American Studies Journal. 11:5-19. Spring '70. New image for the great white father? J. E. Officer.

Montana Business Quarterly. 8:27-30. Summer '70. American Indians in the "melting pot": are Indian communities assimilating into white society? R. J. Bigart.

Nation. 210:496-8. Ap. 27, '70. Who am I? the Indian sickness: the White Hawk case. Roy Bongartz.

Nation. 214:110-13. Ja. 24, '72. Wayne Kennedy case; Chicago Indians supported by AFGE [American Federation of Government Employees] official. Staughton Lynd.

National Journal. 2:1493-502. Jl. 11, '70. BIA [Bureau of Indian Affairs] brings Indians to cities, but has few urban services. J. A. Wagner and Richard Corrigan.

*National Review. 21:223-8+. Mr. 1, '69. Will the Indians get Whitey? John Greenway.

National Review. 25:405-6. Ap. 13, '73. Clean up Wounded Knee.

Nation's Business. 57:76-8. S. '69. Indian country is a frontier again. Prentice Mooney.

Natural History. 79:78+. Je. '70. Indian in America's closet. R. I. Ford.

Natural History. 80:4, 24-33. Je. '71. Watch out, you might assimilate [with biographical sketch]. K. L. Pearson.

*New Leader. 53:13-14. D. 28, '70. Whitewashing the Indians. R. J. Margolis.

New Mexico Business. 23:8-16. N./D. '70. Manpower planning for Navajo employment: training for jobs in a surplus-labor area. Philip Reno.

*New Republic. 168:16-19. Ap. 7, '73. Indians on and off the reservation; from wards to freemen. P. R. Wieck.

New York Post. p 45. Mr. 16, '73. Road to Wounded Knee. Max Lerner.

New York Times. p 26. O. 20, '71. 1970 census finds Indian no longer the vanishing American. Jack Rosenthal.

New York Times. p 43. F. 8, '73. Old Indian refrain: treachery on the Potomac. Les Whitten.

New York Times. p 39. Mr. 20, '73. ... Government of the (white) people. Richard Erdoes.

New York Times. p 39. Mr. 30, '73. That unfinished Oscar speech. Marlon Brando.

New York Times. p 29. Ap. 21, '73. Popularity of American Indian objects soaring. E. C. Burks.

*New York Times. p 14. Jl. 17, '73. Census statistics indicate Indians are the poorest minority group. Paul Delaney.

*New York Times. p 18. Ag. 9, '73. Debris of siege at Wounded Knee is gone but dispute remains. Martin Waldron.

New York Times Magazine. p 47+. D. 7, '69. War between the redskins and the feds. Vine Deloria, Jr.

New York Times Magazine. p 32-3+. Mr. 8, '70. This country was a lot better off when the Indians were running it. Vine Deloria, Jr.

New York Times Magazine. p 26-7+. F. 21, '71. Taos Indians have a small generation gap. Winthrop Griffith.

New York Times Magazine. p 42-3+. O. 17, '71. Natives may win one: great Alaskan real-estate deal. T. M. Brown.

New York Times Magazine. p 18-19+. Mr. 18, '73. Wounded Knee and all that, what the Indians want. A. M. Josephy, Jr.

New Yorker. 46:92+. Ap. 18, '70. U.S. journal: Indian population. Calvin Trillin.

New Yorker. 47:108+. S. 25, '71. U.S. journal: drunken Navahos. Calvin Trillin.

New Yorker. 47:93-7. D. 18, '71. U.S. journal: Tesuque, New Mexico. Calvin Trillin.

New Yorker. 48:28-31. My. 27, '72. Speaks with sharp tongue. Kahn-Tineta Horn.

New Yorker. 49:29-30. Mr. 24, '73. Notes and comment: visit to the Pine Ridge Indian reservation.

Newsweek. 74:28-9. Ag. 18, '69. Village Indian; new commissioner.

Newsweek. 77:94+. Je. 14, '71. Indian in the city: effects of relocation.

*Newsweek. 81:71-2. F. 12, '73. For Indians, by Indians [community colleges on reservations in South Dakota].

Newsweek. 81:27+. Mr. 12, '73. Return to Wounded Knee; Sioux militants' confrontation with federal authorities.

Newsweek. 81:22-3. Mr. 19, '73. Siege of Wounded Knee.

North American Review. 6:56-64. Spring '69. Indian's view of Indian affairs. Joseph (Nez Percé chief, d. 1904).

Parents Magazine. 45:66-8+. S. '70. Failure in Navaho schooling. D. A. Erickson.

Parks and Recreation. 8:28-31. Mr. '73. Indians learn 3 C's: campgrounds, culture, and currency; tourism and campground management training program. J. W. Hanna.

*Progressive. 33:13-17. D. '69; 34:35-9. Ja.; 26-30. F. '70. American Indians. William Brandon.

Ramparts. 8:26-38. F. '70. Red man's burden. Peter Collier.
    Abridged version. Current. 119:22-6. Je. '70.

Ramparts. 9:35-45. S. '70. Theft of a nation: apologies to the Cherokees. Peter Collier.

Ramparts. 11:35-41. D. '72. Alcatraz is not an island; Indian occupation of Alcatraz. Richard Oakes.

Ramparts. 11:10-12. Ja. '73. Bury my heart on the Potomac. E. I. Meyer.

Saturday Review. 53:54-7+. Ja. 24, '70. Time to redeem an old promise. Estelle Fuchs.

Saturday Review. 54:53. Ja. 16, '71. Blazing a new trail; recommendations of the National Study of American Indian education. Susan Boyer.

Saturday Review. 54:44-5. S. 4, '71. First Americans as artists. Katharine Kuh.

Saturday Review of Society. 1:16-17. Mr. '73. Honest Injun: Chief Henry and the tourists. Don Causey.

School and Society. 99:468-9. D. '71. IBM computer for Navajo language textbooks.

School and Society. 100:25-8. Ja. '72. Educational achievement among three Florida Seminole reservations. H. A. Kersey, Jr. and H. R. Greene.

Scientific American. 224:12, 32-42. F. '71. Iroquois confederacy [with biographical sketch]. J. A. Tuck.

Senior Scholastic. 94:13-15+. Mr. 7, '69. American Indians: strangers in their own homeland? [with biographical sketches]

Senior Scholastic. 95:3-7. O. 13, '69. American Indians: the right to be themselves.

*Senior Scholastic. 97:21-3. S. 28, '70. Indian reservations: should they be abolished?

Senior Scholastic. 99:2-7. D. 6, '71. About Indians, by Indians; quotations.

Senior Scholastic. 101:10-11. N. 13, '72. Land they loved and lost: the Menominee Indian story.

Senior Scholastic. 102:8-9. My. 14, '73. Why are the Indians angry?

Seventeen. 32:88-9+. Ja. '73. Among the Navajos: what it's like living on an Indian reservation. Arnold Hano.

Social Forces. 48:243-50. D. '69. Some aspects of American Indian migration. A. L. Sorkin.

Social Science Quarterly. 53:606-18. D. '72. Contemporary perspectives on Indian Americans; a review essay. H. M. Bahr and B. A. Chadwick.

*Social Work. 18:80-6. Ja. '73. White House conference on the American Indian. C. E. Farris.

Society. 10:45-7+. Mr. '73. Indian powerlessness in Minnesota. J. J. Westermeyer.

Southwestern Journal of Anthropology. 27:97-128. Summer '71. Indian reservations, anomie, and social pathologies. J. E. Levy and S. J. Kunitz.
    Bibliography, p 124-8.

Time. 95:14-20. F. 9, '70. Angry American Indian: starting down the protest trail.

Time. 101:18. Mr. 19, '73. Behind the second battle of Wounded Knee.

Times Literary Supplement (London). 71:829-31. Jl. 21, '72. Dispossessed Americans.

Today's Education. 59:24-7. Mr. '70. Indian education: a national disgrace; a dialogue. G. D. Fischer and W. F. Mondale.

Today's Education. 62:39-40+. Ja. '73. What about the first Americans? F. E. Svensson.

*Today's Education. 62:22-4. My. '73. American Indians: beyond the stereotypes. Franklin Ducheneaux.

Today's Health. 48:16-17. O. '70. New Indian war, against suicide. J. L. Bach.

U.S. News & World Report. 69:68-70. S. 14, '70. New deal coming for American Indians?

U.S. News & World Report. 73:109-10. N. 20, '72. Behind the Indians' uprising; what they have, and want.

U.S. News & World Report. 74:36. Mr. 12, '73. Behind a modern-day Indian uprising: Sioux militancy.

*U.S. News & World Report. 74:26-30. Ap. 2, '73. Real goals of the restless Indians.

Vital Speeches of the Day. 36:276-9. F. 15, '70. American Indian [job opportunities]; address, December 9, 1969. Donald Greve.

*Wall Street Journal. p 1+. Mr. 9, '70. Red man's plight: urban Indian, driven to city by poverty, finds harsh existence. Barbara Isenberg.

Wall Street Journal. 178:1+. O. 13, '71. Restless reservation; problem of the Navajos. Hal Lancaster.

*Wall Street Journal. p 26. Mr. 20, '73. At Wounded Knee, is it war or PR? Greg Conderacci.

*Wassaja (national newspaper of Indian America). p 1+. F.-Mr. '73. Wounded Knee seen symbol of resistance. B. C. Mele.

*Yale Alumni Magazine. 36:7-15. O. '72. New old West. H. R. Lamar.